DEEP DISH

DEEP DISH

INSIDE THE FIRST 50 YEARS OF LOU MALNATI'S PIZZA

MARC MALNATI

A Midway Book
AGATE
Chicago

First printed in January 2025

Printed in the United States of America

10 9 8 7 6 5 4 3 2 1   25 26 27 28 29

ISBN-13: 978-1-57284-355-4 (hardcover)
ISBN-10: 1-57284-355-1 (hardcover)
eISBN-13: 978-1-57284-899-3 (ebook)
eISBN-10: 1-57284-899-5 (ebook)

Cataloging-in-Publication Data is avilable from the Library of Congress

Cover image by Tom Molitor
All other images courtesy of Marc Malnati

Midway is an imprint of Agate Publishing. Agate books are available in bulk at discount prices. For more information, visit agatepublishing.com.

For Jeanne,
My eyes continue to sparkle for you, even after 45 years.

FOREWORD

In 1971 when my father opened his first Lou Malnati's pizzeria in Lincolnwood, Illinois, I was eleven. My only sibling, my brother, Marc, was four years older than me. It's crazy to think that after more than fifty years, the restaurant is still going strong!

The average lifespan of a full-service restaurant is less than four years. How did Malnati's survive the death of Lou, the man everyone looked to as their boss and the huge personality that drove the business? How did Malnati's come to grow restaurants in multiple states and to ship pizzas across the country? In *Deep Dish: Inside the First 50 Years of Lou Malnati's Pizza*, Marc gives you an inside look at how that and much more happened in our family business.

Obviously, there are many who deserve credit. The old-time crew that Lou brought with him from downtown were ultra-loyal to him and had years of pizza-making experience. There is the leadership group of people who joined us later and dedicated their entire working lives to the Malnati dream. Also, the many Hispanics, who brought their fierce work ethic. Finally, Malnati's became the first job of hundreds of young kids who would answer the phones, work the cash register, or bus tables. Many of them were gifted in the art of hospitality and eventually worked their way into a management position. We are indebted to everyone who had a hand in the secret sauce!

All that being said, every great company needs a gifted leader, and that person is my older brother, Marc. Leading a company at the young age of twenty-two after your father has passed away looks like a recipe for disaster, but Marc hit it out of the park.

I was fortunate to have had a front row seat for this Malnati miracle. Growing the company was my dad's dream, and though he never had the pleasure of seeing it come to fruition himself, my brother was able to fulfill that dream.

My family is by no means perfect, and the volatility of our younger years created some issues that both Marc and I needed to deal with once we were old enough to tackle them. In all those cases, Marc led the way, and I would follow. He was my protector when I was a kid scared of my dad, he was my cheerleader when I was playing sports growing up, he was my partner once I got out of school, and he will always be my best friend.

This is not a story about great pizza, although we do serve the best pizza in the world. This is a story about how a somewhat dysfunctional family led to the growth of a more functional business family and was blessed by God the whole way. This journey and this book is about that blessing!

RICK MALNATI

1.

Lou Malnati was color TV when the rest of the world was still black and white. As the 1960s turned into the 1970s, Lou was ahead of the fashion curve, flaunting leisure suits with big, flowery, multicolored silk shirts. He wore banana-yellow, lime-green, raspberry-red—one in every flavor. At six feet tall and around 240 pounds, he stood out in a crowd, particularly when he aired his blustery bravado, which expanded when he added Scotch whiskey. And add it, he did. He was the poster boy for Dewar's White Label, and it was not uncommon for him to polish off more than half a bottle and remain generally functional during a shift in his restaurants.

Despite—or, perhaps, because of the whiskey—he was a world-class promoter. He never forgot a face, and he could have anyone, from the guy parking cars to the CEO of a publicly traded company, eating out of his hand in under thirty seconds. He knew everyone, and everyone had a story about a crazy night they had spent partying with their dear friend Lou. His bold-faced name showed up regularly in Chicago's newspaper gossip columns.

Still, Lou's immense talents came burdened with a commensurate handful of flaws. He could take over a room whenever he wanted through the strength of his personality and with his booming Marine Corps staff sergeant voice. Whether telling a joke or sharing a funny story, Lou was the funniest guy in the room. He had a doctorate in facial expressions and loved to make people laugh. But making people cry came just as easily, and if he happened to notice that one of his servers wasn't giving a guest an appropriate amount of attention, Lou's wrath would storm with all the world watching. A hundred customers would stop eating mid-bite and cringe as Sergeant Lou dressed down the hapless waiter.

Lou Malnati was my dad. I was in awe of him and scared to death of him. He could be loving and supportive, but he had a bad temper. Much of that temper was directed toward my mom, my brother, and me. Especially my mom. She received the brunt of his frustration and of his drinking on a regular basis. My only sibling, Rick, is four years younger. He and I were the unseen and powerless audience to their nightly battles. We were like witnesses to an automobile accident who watch helplessly as a car tumbles over the cliff.

But like so many things in life, what doesn't kill you makes you stronger. Sifting through the rubble of my childhood led me to a path of personal growth and emotional recovery that helped to ensure the success of our family's restaurant business. My experience taught me that rocky circumstances can build resilience and character. I learned firsthand that the things that might have been destructive can teach and mold us in a way that would inspire a constructive, new form of leadership.

IN THESE PAGES, I PLAN to tell the story of the first fifty years of Lou Malnati's Pizzerias, a small family business that became the nationally celebrated standard bearer for Chicago pizza, growing to seventy-five restaurants in four states, 3,500 employees, and over $200 million in annual sales. More importantly, it became a company that sought to be more than just another restaurant chain—a company that was built to become a caring, committed community.

Lou Malnati was born in Italy in 1930 and traveled to Chicago as a baby with his mother, Maria Malnati. Her husband, Adolfo, who was affectionately known as Papa to friends and customers alike, had arrived earlier and already become a U.S. citizen. But Maria didn't like the Chicago climate and decided to return home to Italy with her only child. Adolfo remained in the Windy City, working as a bartender at Ric Riccardo's, a popular Italian restaurant opened just after Prohibition on Rush Street in downtown Chicago. Family separations of this sort were typical for Europeans in the 1930s and 1940s, much as they have been for many of the Hispanic families who became the backbone of Malnati's in the 1990s and 2000s. Immigrants would come to the United States, where they would earn a far better wage than in Europe. Their dream would be to work a few years and take the savings back home, though they seldom returned. Life in America was too good!

When Lou was nine, his mother died suddenly on Easter Sunday. Adolfo depended on Lou's two grandmothers to assume the job of raising the boy. They lived in the town of Varese, in Italy's hill country in the north, just outside of Milan. Italians had been eating pizza for centuries, and northern Italy was the home of pan pizza—often known today as deep-dish—a meal that grew out of both necessity and convenience. Northern Italians knew how to bake bread and how to get dough to rise and ferment to add flavor. Lou's grandmothers would add tomatoes, peppers, onions, mushrooms, and, on a good day, some chunks of chicken. It was peasant food, but it was hardy and provided a meal nourishing enough to satisfy the whole family. Growing up, Lou was a good student in the kitchen, though he never realized that this education would serve him well in the next season of his life.

He was also a good student in the classroom and spent a year studying architecture at an Italian college. But with the war over and looking for opportunities, he decided to rejoin his father in Chicago. He arrived in 1947, at age seventeen, not speaking English. To learn the language, Lou attended a North Side Catholic school—beginning in kindergarten! Years later, he recalled his little classmates painting "the big kid" with school paste, the thick creamy kind that some crazy youngsters would eat when the teacher wasn't looking. Lou moved up a grade every few weeks until he became fluent.

At eighteen, he joined the Marines, eventually rising to staff sergeant, and fulfilled most of his time after boot camp running a supply office in Chicago. For extra cash, Adolfo—Papa—got him a bartending job at a new little downtown Chicago restaurant named Pizzeria Uno Riccardo. The place was owned by Ric Riccardo, a savvy restaurateur and part-time artist, who had a silent partner named Ike Sewell, a former University of Texas football star and liquor salesman. A couple of years later, Papa, who had been a mainstay at Riccardo's flagship restaurant a few blocks away, was asked to manage the pizzeria. He and Lou worked side by side there for more than twenty years.

Pizza was just starting to catch on in postwar America, and a handful of pizzerias had opened in Chicago, mostly on the South Side serving thin-crust pizzas. Uno, which started as a little postage stamp of a joint with thirty to forty table seats, served an early variety of pan pizza. In its first years, bartenders would hand out small slices at the bar to inspire liquor sales. This original pizza combined either dough and cheese or dough and sausage (without cheese), both topped with tomato sauce. Over the early years, the pizza evolved under the direction of various people, including Lou. He loved jumping back into the kitchen, as it reminded him of his days cooking with his grandmothers in the old country. Lou saw that people liked it when he would combine the cheese and sausage and when he'd add vegetables—onions, green peppers, and mushrooms—as was done back in Italy. Pan pizza started to enjoy a following of its own. Lou added the personality.

Meanwhile, a young woman named Jean Noll worked as a secretary in an office a block away from the pizzeria. She was a local girl, the daughter of conservative, working-class German parents. Jean had a friendly way about her and connected easily with people. Her father served in the U.S. Army in World War I and worked as a streetcar engineer. Her mother loved the kitchen and could bake like nobody's business. She taught Jean everything she knew.

Jean liked Uno because it was lively, and she was a big fan of the deep-dish. When she stopped in for lunch, Papa, the front man, greeted her with a big, crooked-tooth smile and with his proprietary, "*Ciao, Bella!*" One day Jean brought a date along, and Papa pulled her aside and asked why she didn't go out with his son. When Papa proceeded to make the introduction, both sides showed immediate interest. Lou was working almost every day and drawing on his size to play lineman on a semi-pro football team—a sport he'd picked up quickly from his American friends. Still, he had no trouble making time to go out with Jean. After dating for two years, Lou proposed, and they were married in October 1954. Both were twenty-four. They held their reception at Riccardo's.

Ric Riccardo died that year, leaving his pizzeria in the hands of Ike Sewell. Uno prospered sufficiently that in 1955, Lou and Papa opened a sister restaurant, Pizzeria Due, around the corner, and then in 1963, Su Casa, Chicago's first upscale Mexican restaurant. In 1970, as Lou celebrated his fortieth birthday, he approached Sewell and asked if he could acquire an ownership interest in the pizzerias and Su Casa. After all, Sewell had no children to whom he could pass the business. Sewell told Lou that he loved him "like a son," but he viewed Lou as a manager only and intended to sell the company for big money at some point. Lou quit the next week. He urged his dad to join him, but Papa worried that his son was making a rash decision and chose to stay behind with Sewell. Papa died a few years later, in 1974, but by then he had realized that Lou had made the right move.

After quitting, Lou had to figure out how he would feed his family, but his first impulse was to operate out of spite. He would open on Michigan Avenue, only blocks away from Uno and Due, and show Sewell he had made a terrible mistake. He came close to signing a deal but thought better of it. Instead, he decided to introduce pan pizza to the northern suburbs, where he knew he would have little competition.

His timing was good. The suburbs were growing with the baby boom and the availability of new, affordable housing. After months of searching for a suitable location, Lou and Jean found the perfect spot in Lincolnwood, on the northern boundary of Chicago's city limits. The town offered easy access to the city but featured single-family homes and more space in which to live.

Lou and Jean needed to take on two partners in order to guarantee the lease in Lincolnwood. They required people with sturdy personal balance sheets to ensure their new landlord that the lease would be paid. Lou asked two of his friends from the Shriners, Clare Lang and George Wilson, to cosign. In return, they would each own 25 percent of the business. The restaurant corporation purchased a life insurance policy on them that would provide a handsome payoff should they die before a sale of the business. That was fortunate because Clare passed away unexpectedly soon after the opening, the insurance proceeds going to his estate, and his 25 percent of the business came back to Lou and Jean.

The building they chose was a century old and in an earlier incarnation was said to have been Lincolnwood's first schoolhouse. Lou and Jean decorated the long, rectangular main dining room with an old country Italian theme. Throughout, they stationed oak barrels, a vintage grape press, and straw-covered wine bottles so big you couldn't get your arms around them. A large driftwood sign on the entrance wall welcomed diners. Written in letters fashioned from cork, it read: "*Una cena senza vino è come un giorno senza sole.*" (In English: "A meal without wine is like a day without sunshine.") Lou loved the fact that with 250 seats, his restaurant would be twice as big as Uno and Due put together.

The name of the place was a sure thing, given that Lou was popular with the thousands of customers who had eaten deep-dish downtown: Lou Malnati's Pizzeria. People knew him as a warm, magnetic, jovial guy who had hosted an ongoing party at the bars of Due and Su Casa for twenty years. He was an incredible marketer and a connector of people.

What's more, he had borrowed the twenty-five-year-old loyal customer list from the downtown pizzerias. He realized that many of the customers who worked in the city also lived in the suburbs, so he reached out to them to bring their families to Lincolnwood. After fourteen months of preparation and having whittled away most of their savings, Lou and Jean set opening day for March 17, 1971. An Italian restaurant opening in a predominantly Jewish neighborhood on an Irish holiday. That was their way of trying to welcome people from all walks of life.

Before the grand opening, Lou and Jean held several friends and family nights for the staff to practice pizza service on nonpaying customers. Then Lou threw a monumental press party with a big Italian band. Many local reporters and columnists had congregated at Su Casa with their friend Lou, and he took full advantage of those old relationships to publicize his new venture. Finally, Lou made his signature announcement: "It's time to make the cash register sing!" And sing it did! The line of eager diners outside the front door ran all the way through the parking lot and wound down the street. That first month, sixty to seventy people would be waiting outside when the doors opened each weekday, and the crowd reached hundreds on the weekends.

Lou's courtship of the media paid off handily with mentions in the newspapers. One came from Will Leonard, the *Chicago Tribune*'s popular nightlife columnist, who opened his March 21, 1971, column with a tribute. "Seldom has the lowly but luscious pizza been served in a more attractive atmosphere than this."

Those first several months were exceptionally hectic, and many nights the restaurant felt as if it might burst at the seams. At fifteen, I was put to work, answering the phones and taking carryout orders in the hallway between the dining rooms and the kitchen (school assignments were an afterthought). It was easy to see we didn't have enough workers. New cooks and waitstaff started every day, as workers who couldn't keep up the pace didn't come back. Without a formal training program, Lou had to throw raw employees into the deep end, hoping they could swim.

My parents' friends offered to help with menial jobs and were soon reminded why they hadn't gone into the restaurant business themselves. The scene was often ugly, and I remember seeing my parents beg for forgiveness on a regular basis when we butchered someone's order.

Every new restaurant wants to create a good first impression for all its new guests. One chance is often all a restaurateur gets. But when you're not part of a national chain, and it's your first store, you don't yet have veterans on your staff who understand what it means to be swamped and how to work through it. You can't possibly create a training program that simulates the onslaught that can occur when everyone within thirty miles wants to be the first on their block to kick the tires on the new place. The opening in Lincolnwood was so clunky that by June, my parents took out a half-page ad in the *Tribune* asking people to please give them a second chance!

Besides the activity in the dining rooms, there was lots of action in the little barroom located in the oldest part of the building. The bar at Lou's had a low ceiling that kept the haze of cigarette smoke at about shoulder height on the typical neighborhood eccentric who had claimed a personal stool at the bar where Lou Malnati held court. It was a *Cheers* environment. Everybody knew your name. And the bar was separate enough from the dining rooms that most bar patrons hardly remembered that there was a thriving restaurant just a few feet away. There was Lou Malnati's Pizzeria, and then there was Lou's Bar, which had a reputation all its own.

The bar was U-shaped with low-level lighting that added to its coziness. Lou loved this environment. Having worked for years in Pizzerias Uno and Due, both built in basements with a paltry few dining tables gathered around a prominent bar, he felt right at home. He and Papa had made careers out of managing from their perches at the bar—not behind it—where they could drink, entertain their newest friends, and still see almost everything that was going on. My dad usually sat in the same place, on the bend in the U in his bar chair, which was built with a swivel. Lou reasoned that if you were going to spend as much time as he did at the bar, you needed a chair with a good back. No stools. And that swivel? He needed it to observe everything and everyone. He could talk to people on his right and on his left, watch the bartender in front, and greet the people who came up from behind, while the chair did all the work.

The starting lineup behind the bar included Frank Rueping Sr., a blustery storyteller with whom customers loved to argue history, and Bill Scott, a charismatic full-time bookie posing as a bartender. Although there were frequent celebrity sightings, Lou's bar was dependent on season ticket holders—regulars who often spent more time there than at home or in the office. A long roster of memorable characters filled the ranks, but a few all-stars included:

♦Kenny "The Commissioner" Graebner, who governed all extracurricular competitive exercises, such as football pools and after-hours poker games.

♦Henry "Heintz" Seibel, who was the caddy master at nearby, private Bryn Mawr Country Club. He made it possible for us to be regular Monday golfers when he let us play at the exclusive club on the day it was closed to the members.

♦Joey "Nightlife" Neitlich, a successful marble company owner, who could go hard for hours, pass out as if he were dead while sitting on his stool, and then revive like Lazurus, order a double shot punchino (a coffee enlivened with anisette and brandy) and start his motor up again.

♦John Hamill, who was scolded one late evening by a neighbor for his heavy drinking. "If I was your wife, John Hamill, I would pour arsenic in your coffee," she snarled. The veteran peered at her over his glasses, tapped his cigar, and responded with the well-worn retort, sometimes attributed to Churchill: "Marlene, my dear, if *you* were *my* wife, I'd surely drink it."

My mom paid little attention to the men being boys and trading one-liners with Lou. Although she was a rookie in the restaurant world, she was a quick study. In the early days of Lou's in Lincolnwood, she would run the payroll and pay the invoices that the cheese or sausage vendor presented. She was also a damn good cook. When someone in the kitchen didn't show up, Jean would likely put together a solid lunch special.

Meantime, she wore the hat of both parents. She was far more aware than my dad that they had two boys in school who required parenting. She managed her dual role as Mom and Dad and still usually found a way to work ten hours a day at the new store. Finally, she was the designated driver for Lou each night. Too often, my little brother and I would end up falling asleep in a booth in the bar while Lou told Jean he was going to have just one more.

Having his name on the front door of the restaurant created even more local fame for Lou, and he gloried in it. He believed that the only way to keep his winning streak going was to basically live at his operation. "I'm a restaurant guy. I need the restaurant, and it needs me." I'm pretty sure he was convinced that if he wasn't working, he was cheating his business. That may or may not have been true, but it was what he knew. He would figure out how to attend important family events, such as championship games or graduations, but when it came to the regular dad stuff—such as helping with homework, coaching our teams, fixing our bikes, and such—he wasn't around.

Our family lived in nearby Wilmette when my parents opened Lincolnwood (in Malnati parlance, when we say a town's name, we are always referring to our restaurant in that town and never to the town itself). Being white and upwardly mobile in the 1960s allowed us to attend the best schools. I was a sophomore at New Trier West High School in Northfield. Rick was at Wilmette Junior High.

Up to the point of my dad's exit from Uno, Due, and Su Casa, he had worked Monday through Saturday nights, from 5:00 p.m. until 2:00 a.m. Rick and I were both involved in after-school activities, and our father was long gone by the time we got home at the end of our days. He had only been asleep for a few hours when we left again for school early the next morning. For the most part, we would see him for a few minutes on Saturdays before he went to work, and then on Sunday, when it was his day off. Even then, the entertaining didn't stop. On Sundays our parents usually invited friends over to the house. Lou would stand behind the big stone bar that he had built in our family room, mix drinks, and talk about adult stuff while Rick and I and the children of the guests played in the basement or in the backyard. With the opening of the new restaurant close to home, my brother and I hoped that we would see more of our dad.

That didn't happen—certainly not outside the restaurant—but Lincolnwood did provide me with many indelible memories. One such recollection was the day before my parents opened for the first time, when I got to invite several of my high school buddies into the restaurant to sample the pizza that would take the northern suburbs by storm. For most of them, it was the first time they met Lou. I'll never forget that day. We stood around, a captive audience, as my dad bragged that this would only be the first of several pizzerias he would open in the Chicago area. He brazenly predicted that before he was finished, "Malnati's Pizza" would be a household name. He had gargantuan hopes and dreams for this new venture. And I believed him.

If my friends were to cast the deciding votes, success was all but guaranteed. Lou cut piece after piece out of the steel deep-dish pizza pans. My friends' eyes popped as he raised a slice with his usual showmanship, and the mozzarella stretched like a rubber band. More than half a century later, the memory of eating those first pizzas, prepared by Lou himself, still comes up for Rooth, Richie, Hirschy, Weiner, and me. Nothing ever tasted better.

2.

The magic of our pizza begins with a simple bread dough that we allow to rise twice. We form it, let it rise with air, flatten it, then let it rise again. The dough thus becomes light, delicate, and spongy and takes on a yeasty aroma as it rests, waiting to be patted out in a blackened pan. When it is gently pulled up the sides of the pan, it forms a receptacle in which more goodness can be piled. The bottom is layered with slices of creamy, rich Wisconsin mozzarella made by artisan cheesemakers at the same little dairy since the 1980s. Add lean pork sausage seasoned with more than a hint of garlic. But no fennel. (Lou swore he'd never use fennel. He thought sausage makers who used fennel were just trying to cover the flavor of bad meat.) Sausage remains the most popular ingredient on a Chicago pizza—a reminder that for one hundred years, Chicago was home to the nation's largest stockyards.

Fresh garden vegetables are next in line—onions, garlic, peppers, mushrooms, and, more recently, spinach. Then comes the coup de grâce, peeled pear tomatoes from California. Each summer we send a team of our food experts out to the West Coast near the end of August, where they wait at the plant for the short window of time when the tomatoes have reached their zenith in plumpness and sweetness and have achieved that deep red color—in other words, when they are so delicious that our team members can't stop eating them whole. That's when the team gives the word to can those succulent orbs. Approximately six hours from the time the tomatoes are picked off the vine the perfection is sealed into the number 10 cans. No hothouse tomatoes or flavor shortage here.

Pizza was and always will be the north star of all our menu offerings at Malnati's. Along with pizza, our first menu in 1971 featured a salad, a beef sandwich, a sausage sandwich, and a hamburger. Spumoni for dessert. A small cheese pizza cost $1.50 and a large cheese and sausage $4.00. If you were thirsty, you could get a Coke for a quarter.

As the years went on, the pizza didn't change, but we have learned to monitor the ingredients closely, as subtle alterations in the environment, the weather—climate change!—and even the production plant can affect any individual ingredient and ultimately our pizza. And since the grain for the flour, milk for the cheese, and pork from the pigs are each sourced through living things, pizza will always be a dynamic product that requires regular tiny tweaks to keep it consistent—to maintain the highest quality and the same great taste as we always have. On top of that, we will always need to be advocates for the well-being of farms and the key role they play in our food chain.

Meantime, we have expanded the menu but only when we could deliver an item that could stand on its own. Everything must be fresh and prepared on-site. Even after we had more than thirty stores, we rejected the idea of opening a commissary—a central kitchen for making dough, sauces, and dressings. The thought was that we wanted every kitchen crew in every store to take pride in, and responsibility for, what they sent out to our customers. If the sauce or the dough was made off premises, that might give them a reason to shrug their shoulders when something was not up to the liking of one of our guests.

We were committed to becoming the Mercedes Benz of the local pizza business, believing that if we produced the tastiest and freshest food, our customers would return for more. Pizza was always the award winner, but it was important to have a strong supporting cast of delectable options. Each new dish was brought to life by a different key contributor who loved to experiment in the kitchen.

After a few years of business, we added several pasta choices. The favorite was Penne ala Malnati. Sam Hernandez, Lincolnwood's steam chef for thirty years, started adding butter and cream to Lou's meat sauce, and then slowly melted in little chunks of mozzarella. The dish became an immediate staff favorite. You couldn't find it yet on the menu, but Sam was knocking out twenty-five orders a day just for employee meals. Why would we need to do additional research before offering it to our guests? Once it reached the menu, it was hugely popular.

Our thin-crust pizza debuted in 1987 when Brandon Davies, the manager in our Northbrook carryout store, started passing out little slices. He and his kitchen crew had fallen in love with their rendition of a thin butter crust, and so did their customers as they sampled it when they came to pick up their orders. There was one small problem. He did it without telling me or Rick because he was scared we'd say no. And he was right! But once we tasted the pizza and saw how our guests were receiving it, we introduced it into the other restaurants as well.

Salads were never a focus until about twenty years ago. Today, I think we sell $10 million in salads with house-made dressings every year. Our simple salad with a red wine vinaigrette has stood the test of time. Now we offer a turkey club salad with a tangy BBQ dressing—our take on a bacon, lettuce, and tomato sandwich. But the king of salads is our Malnati salad, with a sweet vinaigrette dressing. Our veteran general manager, Wendy Kolton, and executive chef, Jim Freeland, perfected the dressing, which we ladle over a bed of romaine that has been topped with bruschetta tomatoes, black olives, fresh mushrooms, grilled salami bits, and Gorgonzola cheese.

Ten years ago, we added chicken wings, an appetizer that our catering director, Tony Herrera, worked on for months before it earned a place on the menu. Flavored with either of two sauces—buffalo (Buffalou) or

BBQ (Bar-B-Lou)—our wings are outstanding and have turned into a favorite.

Veteran customers of our restaurants know to save room for the Chocolate Chip Pizza: a freshly baked Toll House cookie with three healthy scoops of Homer's vanilla bean ice cream in a sizzling six-inch pizza pan. (We stole the concept from our friend Tim McGivern at the legendary Great Godfrey Daniels saloon. My parents taught us to give credit even when theft is involved.)

I've named our menu legends, but we are always inventing other dishes that will find their place in our hall of fame. We succeed by sticking to the highest level of quality that we know and preparing our meals in-house. Excellence has been our master from the start. We pay top-end prices for the ingredients, and our vendors know that we have zero tolerance for a drop in quality, because when quality declines, customer counts decline. It's the great law of the restaurant universe.

That is the main reason that we have rarely changed our suppliers over the years. On day one, Lou brought in Frank Battaglia, and the Battaglia family has worked hand in hand with us since then to source our flour, mozzarella, sausage, and tomatoes. The Battaglias have grown their business as we have grown ours, so that now they service our stores in Arizona and across the Midwest. Others among our best and most loyal purveyors include Turano for bread, Sysco for distribution, and Blodgett for ovens. All these world-class companies have partnered with us to create that crucial consistency that can make or break a brand.

3.

ELK GROVE VILLAGE IS A middle-income town in the northwest suburbs with an industrial business base. Aptly named, the village abuts Busse Woods, a county forest preserve that's home to a herd of elk. Lou and Jean calculated that the plethora of businesses and the ease of travel east and west on Higgins Road, which ran through the town, would create a solid foundation on which to build a second restaurant. Even though the Lincolnwood launch eight months earlier had been lumpy, how was Lou ever going to catch Ray Kroc at McDonald's if he didn't move quickly?

The opening party in November 1971 was another wild one. The high point came when Chicago Bears middle linebacker Dick Butkus (and two of his brothers, who were both bigger than the Bear) led the entire gathering, staff and all, around the restaurant in a giant snake of a conga line. Lou had come to know many prominent Chicago athletes during his nights at Due and Su Casa. I recall Cubs coming to our home on Sundays. Even famous New York Yankees, Whitey Ford and Mickey Mantle, used to stop at Due for pizza and to share a drink with Lou when the team was on the road in Chicago.

One of the Bears Lou befriended was halfback Brian Piccolo, who worked his way into the starting lineup beside Gale Sayers until short-ness of breath forced him out of a game. Doctors diagnosed cancer, and Piccolo died months later, in the summer of 1970, at the age of twenty-six. After opening Lincolnwood the following year, Lou and Jean, along with former Bears great Johnny Morris and his wife, Jeannie, put together the first Brian Piccolo Scholarship Dinner.

Our parents always believed they owed a debt to the community that supported their business, and they pledged to give back. Lou closed the restaurant for a night, and the Bears and hundreds of fans celebrated Piccolo's "short season" with a fundraiser, the money going to a college scholarship at Brian's alma mater, Wake Forest University, for a Chicago high school football player. Together with their purveyors, Mom and Dad bore the cost of food, drink, and labor that night. And everybody who was anybody in Chicago sports attended including the Papa Bear himself, George Halas. All the local TV networks showed up to report live from Lou's. *Tribune* columnist Dave Condon broke his rule against mentioning fundraisers and devoted an entire column to promoting the event.

That dinner became an occasion to support cancer research through Northwestern Memorial Hospital in Chicago. Jean has kept what's now known as the Lou Malnati Cancer Benefit going to this day, raising mil-lions over its fifty-plus-year run. No matter what she has had going on in her life, she has carried on the tradition of giving back. My parents' generosity led to the naming of the Lou and Jean Malnati Brain Tumor Institute at Northwestern, recognized as one of the top ten such centers in the world.

Some say there are only two seasons in Chicagoland—winter and construction. Only five months after a strong Elk Grove opening, the county began a project to widen Higgins Road—right in front of the restaurant. That led to noise, dust, huge grinding equipment, and a par-tially blocked driveway. So much for ease of access. Over the next four-teen months, my parents saw revenue at their new store plummet to unsustainable levels. After a year of brutal sales, Lou's accountants told him that he should close the restaurant to avoid bankruptcy. But he had seen potential in those first few months, and he maintained faith that once the road was back to normal, his customers would return. It was an awful waiting game, but his hunch was right, and things began to click again in the summer of 1973. Elk Grove turned the corner and Lou's indomitable spirit was rewarded.

In August of that year, I became the first member of the Malnati/ Noll lineage to attend college. No one on either side had ever earned a college diploma. I chose Indiana University in Bloomington. It was far enough away for me to be independent but close enough to home that I could visit when I wanted. That turned out to be critical, as midway through my freshman year, my mom noticed that a spot on my dad's back had grown and turned dark. Doctors diagnosed a melanoma and decided to operate, taking a chunk out of his upper back and armpit. His recovery included chemo, radiation, and physical therapy, but after six months, doctors reported that he was in remission, with no sign of the cancer remaining.

As Dad began to regain his strength, he started thinking about taking more time to smell the roses. Over the next two years, he and Mom planned an epic trip back to Italy to see his hometown and to visit with his remaining Italian family and old friends. Mom and Dad spent two weeks at Villa d'Este, a picturesque resort on Lake Como. Dad found time for drawing and painting, nurturing his lifelong dream of being the next da Vinci.

He also made time for his sons—for example, making only his second trip to Bloomington to visit me at college for my twenty-first birthday. I felt incredibly happy. We made the most of the weekend, stopping at many of the local saloons, where I no longer needed to use my phony IDs. In his showman fashion, he popped for my crew of twenty close buddies at the Cork & Cleaver, the best steakhouse in B-town. And he bought a round of drinks for every customer in the restaurant so they could celebrate with us!

My dad's energy remained strong enough that in early 1977 he decided to open a third restaurant in Flossmoor, in the suburbs just south of Chicago. But while construction was underway, his cancer returned, this time with a vengeance. Doctors found tumors everywhere. His lymph nodes. His lungs. This time, he lost most of his hair during chemo and immediately looked like he had aged twenty years. He summoned the strength to attend my college graduation in May, but I arrived home a few weeks later to find him on the couch in our living room, breathing with the help of an oxygen tank. He wore pajamas and a robe all day and couldn't go to work. He was wasting away to nothing, and his doctors couldn't do anything about it. With no appetite, he was down to 175 pounds from his normal 240. By winter, friends were starting to stop by the house to see him one final time.

In January Dad was relegated to the cancer ward on the fourteenth floor of Northwestern Memorial's Passavant Pavilion, on the spot where Lurie Children's Hospital now stands. The wonderful nurses there showered him with love and kindness. They even learned to laugh at the raunchy humor that only Lou could get away with. At forty-eight, he was markedly different from the other predominantly senior patients in the cancer ward. So young and so full of life.

One night my mom called with the dreaded SOS. By then I was working at the restaurant in Flossmoor, but I left immediately and drove downtown to the hospital. I found my dad struggling to breathe. His lungs were filling up with fluid, and he was making the rattling sound sick people make when death is near. He was getting oxygen through his nose, and doctors had administered morphine to ease the pain and to calm the fear created when you're drowning in your own internal fluids. It was heart wrenching to stand there, helpless, watching him sleep fitfully with his mouth hanging open. My mom had alerted my brother, who was a freshman at Bradley University in Peoria, attending on a basketball scholarship. He had a game in Carbondale that night but would fly to Chicago early the next morning with the hope to be there in time for his final goodbye.

I slept off and on in a chair in the hospital room. Each time I woke up, I had to face the reality of the approaching end. There were so many things that had gone unsaid between us, so many thoughts and feelings that I had no idea how to express. I'd eventually need to sort it out in therapy, where I'd realize how angry I was at him for not really making the time to know me, for not coaching me, for being a bully, for smoking two packs of Marlboros a day, for the effects of the ever-present Scotch. And because now he wouldn't be there to experience life with me.

Overlaid on my anger, though, was my deep love for him, the love every little boy has for the dad to whom he looks up. I was proud of what he had accomplished, and I longed for him to be proud of me. But in that moment, I was just numb, because going numb was what I had learned to do best.

Of course, I was sad that he was dying, but I also felt guilty, because I was mostly sad for myself. Sad that I would have to become a man and a husband and a father without him walking beside me. And the awareness of that loss cast a pallor over the room and over my life.

Mom was on the second, otherwise unoccupied bed in the room, where she had slept for the last ten days. She was exhausted and had fallen asleep soon after my arrival. At about three in the morning, I heard my dad mumbling and moved closer to his bed. We made eye contact and within a few moments he asked how Flossmoor was doing. I lied and told him that I thought we had stopped the financial bleeding. The truth was that we were getting crushed during the cold January and February months. He told me I was doing a good job and that he was proud of me, and I almost started crying. Suddenly, he seemed to rally with the surge of energy that some people conjure just before death.

In his trademark raspy voice, he said, "When I get outta here, we will open a little place with about forty seats where, every night, we serve only our favorite recipes. And if we are busy enough, we'll close on Saturday and Sunday so we can spend the weekend with the family. There won't be any menus. We cook what we want, and you come and eat it. And we serve everything family style on platters and in big bowls." I told him I loved the idea and suggested that we serve a different flavor risotto every night because risotto was one of the dishes he had taught me to make and stands as one of our family's hall of fame recipes. He responded by naming more dishes—veal scallopine and chicken piccata and ossobuco ..."maybe even beef tenderloin with my signature mushroom gravy with sherry."

As we sat in his hospital room at 3:00 a.m. talking, I could almost taste each dish when we introduced it to our secret menu. I'll never forget the way he smiled at me as we dreamed this dream together. God created a magical little bubble of connection between us that night. It was as rich a gift as I've ever received. I think we shared a few dessert ideas, and then he slipped back asleep, his energy sapped from creating an entirely new restaurant concept in fifteen minutes.

Standing next to his bed, I cried tears of both joy and sadness. He had been semiconscious and full of drugs, but suddenly, miraculously, he had found a moment of clarity to share with me thoughts about the business that had consumed his life and would fill mine as well. I knew in that moment that it was his way of handing things off to me—creating a sweet dream that we could share, knowing that his days of creating restaurants was over. It was now up to me and my brother.

Early the next morning, Rick arrived in time to say goodbye. I'm sure Rick wishes he had skipped the game, but he knew—we all knew—my dad would have wanted him to play. In Dad's last years, and as Rick was playing high-level basketball at New Trier, Dad was always my brother's number one cheerleader. At about ten that morning, February 23, 1978, Dad started choking and could not get enough air. Doctors and nurses streamed into the room and released more sedative into his system. A few minutes later the gargling stopped, and he was gone. The hospital staff graciously gave us time to be alone with him. Mom, Rick, and I hugged and cried and told Dad in whispers just how much we'd miss him. Lou's fight was finally over.

Later that night, as word got out, people began to stop at our house with food. Scott Weiner was the first. He had grown up on our block and is like a brother to Rick and me. His parents both worked, so he was at our house a lot. He enjoyed a special relationship with Lou, who had mentored the three of us in some of life's fundamental areas. Lou may not have taught us how to ride a bike or hit a baseball, but he loved to play card games, and from the time I was seven, he had taught us how to play gin rummy and poker. Lou knew that people in every service-based business worked hard but were often underappreciated. He taught us to recognize their labors, and he provided continuing education on the art of tipping generously.

The next morning, Rick and I walked down the street to the funeral home run by the family of my friend Joe Donnellan and made arrangements for our dad's wake. Mom thought a one-day wake wouldn't allow enough time, so she decided we would greet people all afternoon and evening on Tuesday and again Wednesday afternoon. Everyone had loved Lou, and it seemed as if most of Chicago came to pay their respects. Police had to redirect traffic on Skokie Boulevard after the 200-spot Donnellan parking lot filled. I broke down a few times when friends from across the country showed up unexpectedly. It was good to feel loved amid all the sadness. Heartfelt eulogies were delivered by Reverend Nicholas May and U.S. District Court Judge Abraham Lincoln Marovitz.

In his *Tribune* column, Dave Condon called it "ironic" that Lou died of the same disease that took his friend Brian Piccolo, and wrote, "Time ran out on Lou at the age of 48. In terms of service to his fellow man, though, Lou Malnati got more mileage out of those 48 years than other mortals get from 80."

The whole experience was out-of-body, as no one could believe that Lou was gone. And now my mom was a widow in her forties. She was strong, though depleted after enduring the past year at Lou's side.

I remember listening from another room as she spoke with Dad's attorney in our kitchen on the day of the funeral. He had flown in from out of town that morning. With no sense of timing, he decided to relay to her right then something that he claimed Lou had told him privately—that he, Lou's attorney, should control the business until he thought Rick and I were ready.

Mom would have none of that and told him so in no uncertain terms. "Get the f*#k out of my house! You're done. You're fired! You're not *my* lawyer!" She had let Lou push her around for twenty years, and finally the dam broke. No more being controlled by a domineering man. As I look back, I think she was declaring a new life chapter.

4.

TWELVE MONTHS EARLIER, I WAS running afternoon errands in the lively college town of Bloomington, Indiana, driving down beautiful, tree-lined 10th Street toward Southern Sporting Goods in the downtown business district. After another late night of getting high and throwing darts at the Sigma Alpha Epsilon fraternity house, I hadn't even bothered to hang a wake-up tag for the freshmen pledges, whose job it was to wake me at my requested time. Scheduling my classes early in the morning was genius, because when I woke around eleven, I had none of the angst I might have suffered if going to class was still an option. (Obviously, I was not an ambitious student.) So, this bright, winter day in the middle of my senior year was wide open to possibilities.

I'd decided to shoot over to Southern Sporting Goods after lunch and have my racquetball racket restrung with cat gut for a match that evening. I loved this store—an antique combination that featured sporting goods and a soda bar. The place rightfully belonged in Mayberry. The thick chocolate shakes were made in big, stainless steel mixing containers, and you had another half shake left in the container after they served it.

I had my mind set on enjoying one of those shakes while they restrung my racket, when I suddenly recalled that I had committed to attend a meeting—a gathering with eight other presidents from the larger fraternity houses on campus. The meeting was supposed to start in about three minutes. What to do?

A week earlier, Tom Barrett, the director of the Campus Crusade for Christ at IU, had visited my frat house, uninvited, to ask me a few questions about heaven, God, and Jesus. I didn't have much to say—my family was far from religious. My idea of the afterlife was the party that broke out in Red Tuohy's room following a major kegger. As Tom and I talked, guys kept coming in and out of my room, looking for pot, asking if I wanted to get high or if I had seen the stolen econ test. Tom, who had graduated from college a few years before, was undeterred. He asked me to attend a leadership seminar he was putting together at the Acacia fraternity house the following week. I wasn't really interested, but I told him I would go—the truth is, I thought that was the only way I could get him to leave.

Hey, it was my senior year in college. I had succeeded in doing the bare minimum scholastically to eke out a GPA just slightly over 2.0, which maintained my enrollment. And I already had plenty of things on my plate without setting aside time for intellectual or spiritual pursuits. I was trying to win the fraternity racquetball championship after being denied the past two years. I was coaching our Little 500 bike team for the campus race that would be made famous in the 1979 movie *Breaking Away*. And as president of our fraternity, I now supervised the construction of the new basketball court we had talked our alumni into buying for us. I was busy!

But just as I pulled up to Southern Sporting Goods, a loud internal voice rang out. "Marc! You committed to that Tom guy. You said you'd be there." The voice piled on the guilt, saying it wasn't only my reputation, but, as president of SAE, I might also be soiling the fraternity's name. Then something crazy happened. My car backed out of my parking space and turned toward the Acacia house! I started sweating. I heard a voice saying quite insistently, "You need to go to that meeting." I peeked in the rearview mirror but didn't see anybody else in the car. Looking back now, I think I experienced what Tom called a God moment. God whispering that it was time for me to shift—to change the direction of my life.

I arrived a few minutes late to the Acacia house meeting, where Tom led us through conversations that were life-altering for me. No, I didn't immediately lose interest in partying or racquetball or any of the other crazy elements of my college experience. But after that meeting, I began to become more curious about the bigger questions life can pose. Tom had asked several, such as: Is there really a God? If so, does He care about you? Is there a heaven? Or is life over when it's over? Two of the most pressing questions, I secretly asked on my own: What will happen to my dad, who has stage IV lung cancer? And if he's gone, what will happen to me?

Until that point in my life, I had only attended church four or five times. The Catholic Church had alienated my dad when he returned to the U.S. at seventeen. He didn't yet speak English, and a Chicago priest denied him confession in Italian. Because of that, Dad held a grudge and never went back. My mom's family was more spiritually focused, but she hadn't continued as a regular churchgoer. Our family slept in on Sundays. In the months after Tom's meeting, however, as I graduated and returned home, I knew on some unconscious level that my previously nonexistent spiritual life was about to change quite dramatically. I decided to meet again one-on-one with Tom, and he quickly became a guy I believed I could trust.

He led me into the Bible and explained it in a way that made the words come to life. I prayed with him and asked Jesus to be my savior, because I knew I needed Him on my side, especially with the uncertainty that the future held. What's more, I had a warehouse of things for which I needed to be forgiven. It seems I'd been stockpiling them.

5.

DURING AN IMPROMPTU FAMILY BUSINESS meeting that summer, as we gathered around the living room couch where Lou was spending his last days, we decided that I would move out of our house and get a place near our newest restaurant in Flossmoor. That way, I could essentially live in the store, just as Lou would have done if he were able. Sales had looked promising at first, but then the operation fell into a nosedive. We were about to find out that the future of the entire business was at stake, because one bad restaurant can lose money at a far faster pace than two good ones can earn it. And Lou wanted to get his legacy back on track more than he wanted me to live at home and watch him slowly slip away.

I moved to Griffith, Indiana, in August 1977, to share an apartment with my fraternity brother, Pete Crumpacker. Griffith was only about twenty minutes from Flossmoor. Pete worked days and I worked nights, and we barely saw each other because I was in the restaurant eighty hours a week. I was determined to save the venture by riding out the sales dip and turning things around. I needed to prove that I was capable. That I could be successful. That I could be like Lou.

What I would learn in Flossmoor is that we had basically written an infallible business formula:

HOW TO OPEN A RESTAURANT THAT FAILS!

Open in a bad site where you have zero name recognition. The Floss-moor restaurant sat in the middle of a strip mall and had little street presence. Nobody knew it was there. The giant housing development earmarked for the fifty acres of farmland across the street—a project that would break ground "any day now," the landlord assured before Lou signed the lease—would soon be put on hold indefinitely. What's more, South Siders had grown up on thin-crust pizza, and they weren't flocking to sample our deep-dish product. Home Run Inn, Aurelio's, and Vito & Nicks were the Lou Malnati's of Chicago's South Side. The wave of popularity we had experienced when opening the doors in the two north suburban spots didn't develop in Flossmoor. Pick a bad site, and you can seal your fate before you ever sign the lease.

Open so far away from your existing store that your experienced staff can't help you. Flossmoor sits fifty miles away from our restaurants in Lincolnwood and Elk Grove Village. From the start, the distance created issues for training. Prospective staff who lived near Flossmoor didn't want to drive fifty miles north every day to learn a new job. With his severe health issues, Lou didn't have the energy for the drive back and forth to Flossmoor, and especially not to bust balls on the floor and in the kitchen to make sure everyone knew exactly what he wanted. Nor had he been able to convince many of his core team to move to Floss-moor or even travel there. He was forced to hire new managers who struggled from day one. He remembered the mess during the opening in Lincolnwood, but he realized too late that he had pushed his param-eters too far. Outside of a few cooks who lived in the Flossmoor vicinity, veteran employees would have to endure a hundred-mile round trip pil-grimage to work there. Some of Lou's vets came for a few days over the first few weeks. But too soon the rookies were on their own.

Change the way you've made your product for thirty years. Our equipment professionals maintained that since the South Siders were used to ordering thin-crust pizza, which cooks much faster than deep-dish, Lou would need to cook his pizza faster to compete. My dad was not a guy who fixed things that weren't broken. But the equipment vendors convinced him—perhaps because he was weak from illness—and he switched from the gas ovens he had used for nearly thirty years to faster, electric ones. Bad idea. Really bad.

He bought the new ovens from Bakers Pride at double the price. They were beautifully appointed with shiny, stainless steel doors and built to last. They could hold heat and operate more efficiently than our traditional Blodgett gas ovens. Our pizza would come out looking perfect on top when the veteran cooks sent it to the dining room. Minutes later, it returned to the kitchen after diners complained that the bottom was burnt black.

As with a burnt piece of toast, scraping off the black doesn't remove the burnt taste. Believe me, we tried. The equipment people adjusted things, the factory reps came out. After all the tweaking, the ovens worked better, but every time the infrared coils cycled onto "heat," the pizzas would still burn.

Our veteran cooks were frustrated, too. With the electric ovens, the cooks had little time to create pizza perfection—the golden-brown underside and rim, the hint of browning over the bubbling mozzarella and sprinkling of parmesan. If you're a new customer, once you've been served a burnt, black-bottomed pizza, no matter how delicious it might look on top, you don't rush back for more.

Fixing our oven problem wasn't as easy as just switching back to the old standard. A gas oven requires a giant hood that penetrates the kitchen roof. We would have had to close down for at least a week to install the hood, and we couldn't afford the lost revenue, any more than we could afford to buy all that new equipment.

Follow the first three steps of this formula, and you are almost certain to fail before you even open. But certainty comes after you've reduced your weekly revenue to an unfathomable low point and added the fourth and final element.

Bring in an inexperienced twenty-two-year-old general manager to make things right. Flossmoor's new general manager had been out of college for twenty minutes, didn't know his ass from a hole in the ground, and had no clue what his next move needed to be. Me.

When I first arrived, I noticed we weren't doing things the same way as in our other restaurants. The differences ranged from how we greeted guests to how we set tables to how we made salads to how we operated our carryout area. Because of the lack of customers, none of the tipped staff was making enough money to get by. I was continually bringing in new waitstaff, the only exceptions being a few kind, older women. They stayed longer than they should have because they felt sorry for me.

That's the four-step formula. I joke now, but the lessons I learned, though painful, paid dividends later in my life. If I had walked into a restaurant that was busy and firing on all cylinders, it would have been less stressful, but it wouldn't have provided me with my first real-life business education. I wouldn't have realized that failure is a better teacher than success.

I had been in Flossmoor for about six months when my dad died. After the funeral, I doubled down on trying to revive the store, which led to even bigger mistakes. We weren't doing much of a lunch business, so I decided not to open until four in the afternoon, Tuesday through Sunday. To shave costs to the bare bone, I told my two assistant managers that I couldn't pay them any longer and had to let them go. I figured that I could handle the six nights on my own and be there to make sure every pizza went out perfectly. Only after I'd made the changes did I ask the purveyors to push their delivery schedules into the late afternoon. Most of them said they couldn't do it. I ended up having to be there for morning deliveries myself three days a week.

That schedule was brutal for the next three months, and at one point, I ended up in the hospital for an emergency appendectomy. Clearly my body was reacting to stress. Recovery was slow because my appendix had begun to burst, and I had to beg one of the old managers I had recently fired to come back for a few days because I had no backup. Four days in the hospital gave me time to think.

The last thing I wanted was to quit fighting for the restaurant to become successful. My dad had waited out the road construction in Elk Grove, so didn't it make sense to believe that this one could eventually prosper, too? Wouldn't Lou have waited it out? I wanted so badly to make it work for him. I still needed him to be proud of me, even though he was gone. I felt as if he were watching me, and I needed to show him that I was cut out of the same cloth as he was. I needed his team to believe in me and know that I would run through walls to keep this store afloat. Flossmoor had had my full attention, every minute of every day.

The next week, I limped to breakfast with my mom and Virgil Carter, an old friend of our family who was willing to shoot straight with me. We met in the gigantic lobby restaurant of the Hyatt at Illinois Center. I recoiled when he said he thought it was time to shut down Flossmoor, time to make sure that the rest of the company survived. He said he thought we were at a major inflection point, and that if we didn't make the next right move, we could lose everything.

As he said it, I felt waves of sadness. But I didn't resist. I knew he was right. His counsel was not what I was seeking, but it was exactly the counsel I needed to hear. The restaurant business is difficult—only one in ten make it to a five-year anniversary. Lincolnwood and Elk Grove were slightly past the five-year mark, but with the disaster that was Flossmoor, the fledgling Lou Malnati empire was hanging on by a thread.

Over the next two weeks, I began planning for us to move out. Because we were afraid of getting into a skirmish with the landlord, we decided to remove all our equipment, furniture, and smallware unannounced, like thieves in the night. We brought in a team of ten well after dark to load two full trucks, which drove away at five in the morning. After a few hours of sleep, I had to start calling to tell staff members that they were out of a job. People either cried or screamed at me. And I deserved their anger. Closing without warning, leaving them high and dry. People who had depended on me to support their families. I couldn't stand myself. I was young, but I'd already reached what would be the low point in my life as a businessman—and as a human being. We had accrued over a half million dollars of debt in the eighteen months that Flossmoor was open. In today's dollars, that would be more than $2.5 million, and with only two restaurants, we were faced with digging ourselves out of an almost impossible hole. Each restaurant was created as a separate legal entity, and we could have filed for bankruptcy protection in Flossmoor without having to bankrupt the others, but we never considered doing that. The people we owed were purveyors with whom my dad had dealt for years, beginning downtown. They still serviced our two other restaurants. How could we ever face them if we told them we weren't going to pay for the mistake we had made in Flossmoor? Instead, we asked for their patience, and we promised they would get their money back in full if they would give us some time. Then we all prayed it would happen.

Once we closed Flossmoor, I took time off. I needed to recover—physically from the appendicitis attack, emotionally from my dad's death. Plus, my ego would require some healing from the defeat in the Flossmoor debacle. I had bought a little house for $36,000 in south suburban Homewood, planning to live there a long time. I spent a month there alone, mindlessly painting the exterior. I knew I'd be selling it and moving back up north to live in my mom's house and work in Lincolnwood again.

I still felt terrible about the workers who had trusted us and now were scrambling to find jobs. With only two other restaurants, we had nowhere to place them. Besides, the other restaurants were fifty miles away. I felt the worst for several talented cooks, Juanita, Ruthie (creator of our butter crust), and Ruthie's daughter Vera. They had followed my dad from downtown to Lincolnwood to Elk Grove, and, with the opening of Flossmoor, they'd finally been able to work near their homes in Harvey. They must have felt devastated. I had betrayed them by not reopening roles in one of the other restaurants. Ruthie and Vera moved out of state, and I never saw them again. But I ran into Juanita at a funeral several years later. She wouldn't even look at me.

I was twenty-three years old and I felt like I was seventy-three. I was tired and I was sad. Likely depressed. And I was doubting myself like at no other time in my young life. The questions paraded through my head again and again: Was I cut out to run a successful restaurant? Could I lead? Would people ever want to follow me again? I knew I had worked my butt off to revive Flossmoor. I had put in astounding hours. But in the end, we had to lock the doors. Was my best not enough? A nasty little voice haunted me: "Lou would have been able to turn the ship around, but you couldn't. You're a failure."

Soon enough, I'd have to walk back into the Lincolnwood bar with my tail between my legs. I could hear the regulars whispering over their cocktails, "There's the college kid who thought he was really something, but turned out to just be another guy who was born on third base and thought he had hit a triple." And: "Without Lou, this business is in all kinds of trouble. Watch him mess up *our* place now."

I didn't want to find out that they were right.

My house in Homewood wasn't large, but the cedar shake had deep grooves that required painting the whole thing with a brush. After about a month of slow, frustrating progress, I had eliminated painting as a career choice. Because I hadn't drawn a paycheck since I closed the restaurant, I was almost out of money. I didn't want to head up north, but I didn't have an option My body had recovered, but I was still emotionally raw.

How would I silence the voices? Would I have the courage and perseverance to move past this failure? Would I be able to preserve this business that Lou and Jean started? I had started to follow a more spiritual path, and I wanted to believe that God was going to be there to support me, hoping He wouldn't abandon me too.

I forcefully shifted myself into "Go," packed up enough stuff for two weeks, and returned to the house in which I had grown up.

6.

ABOUT THE TIME I MOVED back home, my mom saw an article in the newspaper announcing a music festival called ChicagoFest that Mayor Michael Bilandic planned to stage at Navy Pier. The pier had been devised as an appendage protruding from Chicago's lakefront by Daniel Burnham in 1916 and served multiple functions over time. It had been shuttered since last being utilized as a branch campus for the University of Illinois in the early 1960s.

By 1978, despite the countless broken windows and birds nesting throughout the infrastructure, none of the hundreds of thousands of Chicagoans or tourists seemed to notice as they packed the pier for ten days. Lake Michigan and the Chicago skyline created a beautiful and welcoming backdrop, and sixteen unique music stages featuring acid rock to disco breathed new life into the worn-down venue. Over the six years that ChicagoFest ran, stars like Frank Sinatra, the Beach Boys, Lionel Richie, Carole King, and Journey were headliners.

But as that first ChicagoFest approached, my mom could sense I needed a little win to get back on track, and she suggested that we apply to be food vendors. When I first read the article, I was thinking that this would be a great place to hang out with friends for ten days and zone out. Mom knew best. I applied, not imagining that we would ever be selected, but in late June we received confirmation that we were in. Little did I know what effect that would have on the building and shaping of our company's culture, as well as providing the extra money we needed to repay our purveyors the debt we owed them for Flossmoor. The lessons we learned and the friends we made participating in ChicagoFest on Navy Pier, followed a few years later by Taste of Chicago at Grant Park, and later, Lollapalooza, brought some of the most incredible blessings of our lives.

Creating a festival on Navy Pier or on Columbus Parkway in the middle of Grant Park was a herculean feat for the City of Chicago. There were so many moving parts and nowhere to move. The stands were pint-sized and basically on top of one another. A fast, temporary setup required tremendous coordination and 100 percent cooperation by every restaurateur involved. An entire sanitary village had to be constructed and torn down again over a short period of time. Propane gas, electricity, and potable water and ice were critical, and occasionally temperamental in a makeshift setting with temperatures often climbing into the nineties.

Competitive to a fault, Rick and I determined that we would show Chicago who had the best pizza in town. Our strategy added complexity but made the results monumentally better. We hauled fresh buckets of dough early every morning to the pier, cutting it and letting it rise in the pan. We parked a refrigerated truck on site with thousands of pounds of fresh mozzarella and our famous sausage. We lifted in four 1,400-pound Blodgett gas ovens with a combined sixteen cooking decks, so that we could bake everything fresh, right there on-site for people to see. Making our pizzas from scratch made us battle to keep up with the demand all day long.

As each night ended at 10:00 p.m., our crew was filthy. Uniforms that had begun the day as standard restaurant issue whites were black from the grime and wet from tomato sauce and sweat. After twelve to fourteen hours on our feet, we finished the night bleaching everything down, especially the well-worn concrete floors of Navy Pier. Everyone smelled like a bad combination of perspiration and parmesan cheese as we headed toward our hotel across the street.

We didn't have credit cards or payment wristbands at festivals back then, so I carried the cash in my backpack, through the throngs of party goers celebrating another beautiful evening on Chicago's lakefront. The money looked and smelled as bad as we did. Beer-soaked singles from our adjacent beer stand, uncounted and crinkled up, had been thrown into the backpack and stuck together in a big, wet pile. As we exited with upwards of $25,000 in cash on many nights, we were unlikely targets—a thief would have had to rub up against the filth to steal anything. And who would ever suspect these young, dirty festival workers had any money? Nonetheless, for safety's sake, we always passed along a few hot pizzas to the cops stationed near our stand, and they escorted us out of the venue late at night. Back at the hotel, we'd take thirty-minute showers, order room service, and spread the cash over the floor. We'd count the money between bites of our burgers and fries, because so often we worked like dogs all day, forgetting to stop and eat. Such is the life of most restaurant people I know. Spend your whole day and night serving food and never stop to eat!

One thing was for sure: Our company's work ethic was built on those sweltering streets of downtown Chicago. Out where the asphalt could hit 140 degrees Fahrenheit on cool days and get so soft under the sun that it would begin to swallow up the wheels on our ovens as if it were quicksand. We have worked like that at those festivals from 1978 until the present day.

Under those conditions, we adopted the belief that we could work longer and faster than should be humanly possible and the understanding that doing it together, as a team, would create an unbreakable bond. These tenets became foundational to our culture. Whether at a festival or in our busy restaurants, we reasoned that if people did not have that fifth gear available for them to shift into, if they didn't have something in reserve that they could summon when we were working shorthanded or when the whole city decided to eat at exactly the same time, they could still have a career in the restaurant business—it just wasn't going to be with us.

I saw Malnati's pizza as a sort of underdog in those early years. We weren't going to be happy unless we were selling the best pizza at the best value to our customers and doing more sales than every other vendor. Even if the other vendors weren't competing with us, we were competing with them. We used that mentality to push ourselves every day.

We loved it when we'd notice someone walking by our stand eating a slice they had just purchased from another vendor. We'd watch their eyes for the "Oh, shit" moment. The moment when they realize that they blew it and that if they had only waited a few seconds longer, they would have seen our stand before making their lunch decision. I loved to tell them that if they would throw our competitor's half-eaten slice into the trash, we would give them a beautiful, new slice of our pizza for free. I've never had anyone say no.

Here's how the team would operate at festivals once the rush hit, and we began to crank: The ovenman, who was Pedro or Eloy or Mick or Haddie, would grab a stack of twelve blackened, oily pans, pull it up against his chest, run to an open oven drawer, and start flying the pans into the oven so he could get the door shut without losing too much heat. He had to be an expert at cooking the pizzas fully, perfectly. He'd then turn and begin unloading another oven, reaching his arms into the 550-degree heat, pretending it's not painful as he banged his wrists on the top of the deck, singeing his skin instantly.

The pizza sizzle is closer to a growl at this point, and the ovenman would use a pan clamp in each hand to double stack and carry the smoking 'zas to the cutting table, four at a time. Then he'd dip his hands in the bleach water and reload the empty drawer.

And do not run out of pizzas! Only rookies run out. At capacity, we can put out over eight thousand slices on days when park attendance climbs to over a half million festgoers.

The role of the other thirty to forty workers in the stand is to keep going and never stop, so those ovens stay full. Our sprints could last for four hours or more! The people cutting and weighing dough balls, the people placing slices of cheese on the newly patted dough, the veterans who apply that healthy helping of ground pork sausage evenly and quickly after so many years of experience. The people on the sauce table who finish the pizza preparation a dozen at a time, getting the chunk tomato sauce and whole tomatoes to top the pizza evenly, and finally christen each with that blend of parmesan and oregano.

Once the ovenman pulls the screaming hot pizzas from the oven, the flipper pops them out of the pan with a quick flick of the wrist and the cutter divides each of the nine-inch beauties into four lip-smacking slices. We relished the moments when hundreds of customers begging for a slice of pizza would be shoulder to shoulder across the face of our stand as our sellers plated the slices and handed them off to folks who were watching in awe at the energy they saw being expended in this tiny stand to create the freshest, tastiest pizza on the planet.

Other pizza vendors may be cooking their pizza off-site, boxing it up, and wheeling it in on carts, only to warm it up for a few minutes and serve it. But at Malnati's, we are constantly building our brand, and Lou declared from day one that we won't serve it if it can't be served fresh and hot right out of the oven.

Selling thousands of slices of pizza at a festival can provide a decent day of sales, but winning a thousand people over for life can build a brand. And we're about building a brand, one mouth at a time.

We loved it when we noticed other restaurant workers standing in front of our stand looking on in amazement at how hard our crew was working and secretly wanting to be on our team. If approached, we had some simple questions for potential team members:

+How are you in crunch time?

+Can you work as if you have four hands?

+Do you love the way your body feels when you're operating on pure adrenaline?

✦Can you burn yourself repeatedly and laugh through it?

✦Can you laugh at the craziness of being ridiculously busy and have fun doing it?

If you answered yes to all of these, you clearly have issues, but you're a perfect fit for Malnati's!

Those early events led to some long-term relationships that would have a powerful impact on the company. There was a stocky guy with black curly hair and a mustache with the accounting firm of Bernstein & Banks that ran the money part of the festivals for the city. Always friendly and helpful, smarter than he wanted you to think, Stuart Cohen was the number two in command for Bernstein at the festivals. We liked him enough that Rick and I hired Stu and his company to do the accounting for Malnati's. A few years later, in 1985, he left his opportunity to become a partner in his prestigious firm to join us as our partner and future company president. More on Stu later.

We were selling slices of pizza for $1.50, while Kevin Brown, the manager at Lettuce Entertain You, the hugely successful Chicago restaurant company founded by Rich Melman, was selling ribs for $4. I loved that we were pulling in about the same sales dollars at festivals, while we sold our pizza for less than half the price of ribs. Our friendship began with me giving Kevin the business about how our team kicked his team's butts, how our team outperformed his team all day long. Years later, Kevin, who became the CEO of Lettuce's vast empire, is a trusted friend who sits on our board of directors.

Marc Schulman from Eli's Cheesecake, a festival mainstay, became one of our first partners on our Tastes of Chicago e-commerce site. I met Dan Rosenthal from Arnie Morton's restaurant group at ChicagoFest, and Dan became a friend and sounding board for years. An accomplished restaurateur in his own right, Dan opened several revered Chicago restaurants, including Harry Caray's, Trattoria No. 10, and Sopraffina in downtown Chicago.

Finally, there was a South Side kid named Mike Archer, who flipped burgers for Arnie, then studied finance in college, and later became president of Morton's at only thirty-one years of age. He certainly noticed how much we loved working hard at Malnati's and how we would do whatever it took to get the job done. He must have bookmarked those memories for a later date, because Mike would become CEO of Malnati's in 2020.

At the festivals, there were no breaks during crunch time. I'm not a big fan of breaks. Breaks aren't refreshing. They make you tired. If you take a break, you don't feel like going back to work. Especially if you sit down and eat. It's not that you don't want to take a break or that you're not hungry, it's just that team players discipline themselves not to need breaks when others are depending on them. They are never willing to let their team down. People who take breaks during crunch time typically aren't great workers. People who take breaks have trouble finishing. Team players know how to push themselves until the job is done. And if you are able to keep it in fifth gear at a festival, the bonus is that you never have to visit the porta-potty because you can't drink as fast as you sweat.

When we finally make it through the four-hour-long rush, we get to taste true camaraderie, the "knowing" that occurs when we look at one another and shake our heads, knowing we'll never be able to fully describe what it was like to work that hard to people who hadn't experienced it for themselves. We'll never be able to explain how special it felt to be a part of accomplishing something that seemed nearly impossible, but we stuck together, we did it *with* and *for* one another, and we made it!

Almost like summiting Everest! That's what it feels like to be part of an incredible team.

Having a great work ethic typically goes hand in hand with the need to be part of a great team. Part of a team that is passionate about serving others and that loves to work together. If I love what I do, I want to surround myself with others who love it as much as I do because I know they will make me better, and it will certainly be a lot more fun. I want to be matched. I want to be pushed—I want to be part of something remarkable.

I've become a student of people and the way they work over fifty years of working at festivals and busy restaurants. In tight quarters, you can pick out the teammates who make those around them better. You will see those who are willing to do two jobs at once and those who need to take a cigarette break. To build a company like ours, the underpinning, the very foundation needs to be built on people who will "bring it" and who will teach others to bring it as well. As my brother says, the restaurant business does not require rocket scientists, or he and I would have failed miserably. But it does require loyalty. It's a game of repetition and sacrifice that only happens when people dedicate their careers to one thing and to one another.

I watched Kim Swanson, who would later become one of our district managers and a phenomenal recruiter of future leaders, scrape the carbon off our pans for six hours straight. On her birthday. I'd have to fight Mick Milliken or Eloy Garcia to get them to give up the pizza clamps when they were so exhausted they could barely walk anymore. I've never seen anyone throw fifty seventy-five-pound dough buckets on and off a refrigerated truck at one time like Steve Haddon. I caught Jaime Solis secretly self-administering insulin shots behind our booth while he patted dough with his other hand.

We recognize that we don't have to talk about how good we are. The devotion to one another, to our product, and to the Lou Malnati name on the T-shirts we wear does the talking for us. Like the New York Yankees in their heyday, we outwork everyone else and raise the bar to a level at which others have to compete. There is an outward humility, but we've earned the ability to walk with a swagger.

Even our friends who came out to help us in the early days quickly knew if our stand was a place where they would flourish or where they'd fail. Some even paid a price for showing up. One day in Grant Park, our leadership team coach, Rich Blue, needed twenty-two stitches in his head when a drunken festgoer delivered a closefisted brass knuckle punch to his head.

7.

IN ADDITION TO PROVIDING A welcome bundle of cash, expanding our brand, and creating a valuable sense of camaraderie, our festival experiences produced some memorable moments.

One came on July 3, 1984, at Taste of Chicago, the city's celebrated food festival. On that lovely day, the magnetic aroma of pizza dough, blending with the sweet smell of BBQ, wafted on the warm summer breeze across Chicago's lakefront. The cloudless sky made an idyllic backdrop for the festival in Grant Park. Hundreds of thousands of partygoers shared the grass and shade, the majesty of Buckingham Fountain, the half dozen soundstages featuring a range of musical acts, and dozens of stands offering a cornucopia of foods of all varieties. The day would climax with a world-class fireworks show, the cherry on top of Chicago's largest summer festival. People of all ages and from every country in the world attended. Some dressed like Elvis, some hardly dressed. Families, friends, pickpockets, and mimes. Every demographic you could name and some that defied naming.

This was our fifth year at the Taste, and the day before Independence Day was typically our biggest sales opportunity of the ten-day event. We had every detail fine-tuned. Having learned from past mistakes, we knew we needed to prepare Plan B's for everything that could go wrong when preparing food in the middle of the packed and crowded park. We had extra ingredients in the refrigerated truck and two alternate paths to get food from the truck to the stand as the crowd grew dense. We stocked extra propane, extra water, and extra lengths of the nylon rope that tied the counters to the stand and the stand to the spikes driven into the ground. At some point that afternoon, thousands of people would be pushing their way toward fresh pizza, and those counters were our only protection.

By 1:30, lunch was moving along at a decent clip. We had eight smiling cashiers stretched along the twenty-foot front of our tent and each faced a line of customers. Suddenly, a young, overserved guy wearing baggy camouflage pants, a tank top, and a stupid grin breached our barrier and appeared in the middle of our stand. I told him he couldn't remain and pointed toward the exit. He got belligerent and bellowed, "F*#k off!" Someone confronted him and he started shoving. My friend Rich Blue, five-foot-eight and 245 pounds of mostly muscle, was helping at the stand, and he intercepted the drunk, pinning his arms, and frog-marching him out.

But in a flash, the guy pulled a set of brass knuckles out of his pants pocket and cracked Rich over the head. Rich reacted like the former rugby all-star that he was. He grabbed the drunk's arms, compressed him into a ball, and lofted him through the stand like a misfired missile. The human rocket landed on the prep table, collapsing it, then slid into a pile of bulging trash bags in the beer stand next door. Still, the dumbass wouldn't quit. He advanced toward our ovenman, Marc Miller, who had run over to back up Rich. Finally, my brother and several other of our biggest guys wrestled the jerk to the ground. The police arrived, just as I heard Miller screaming that he wanted to insert the trespasser into his 550-degree oven.

I had heard about brass knuckles, but I don't think I'd ever seen a set up close, and I'd certainly never seen the weapon deployed. The drunk refused to surrender them, so one of the officers took out his billy club and smashed every finger on the man's hand. The cops cuffed the guy and hustled him out. Meanwhile, Rich Blue felt blood running down his face and on the back of his head. His scalp had been torn open like a fresh can of tomatoes.

In some counterintuitive way, the pandemonium may have been just what we needed heading into a record-setting evening. Our people now had an edge. I've never been in a real war (and I don't mean to minimize the fact that in a real war, our troops lay their lives on the line), but we were in our own version of a foxhole, sardined in the middle of the park, willing to do whatever it took to protect one another. Our own little Band of Brothers.

I brought Rich to the medical tent, but the attendants said his wound was too extensive to close in their remote facility. We'd need to get him to Northwestern Memorial Hospital, which was only about a mile away. But Columbus Drive and all the surrounding streets were closed to vehicles. A nearby police captain had heard about the incident with the "knucklehead," and he told us to get in his squad car. Siren blasting, lights flashing, screaming over his PA system for people to get out of the way, he drove the wrong way on streets and down narrow sidewalks on the way to the ER. In the back seat, Rich and I laughed like kids on a roller coaster and held on for dear life. I told Rich it was worth getting stitches to get a ride like that. He just slugged me in the ribs.

Brandishing twenty-two new stiches, Rich was back with us in the stand before the dinner rush.

Though during most of our time at festivals we worked like mad, we still found creative ways to amuse ourselves. Occasionally, our laughs came at someone else's expense, especially if we felt that a certain someone needed a lesson on hubris. One such episode took place when a local health department official—let's call him O'Brien—walked into our stand in the middle of the lunch rush to complete what should have been a routine inspection. We had worked with this agent before and knew that he could be grouchy. We followed all the refrigeration rules to the letter, and with ovens set at over 500 degrees in 90-degree weather, we never had a problem getting our pizzas up to 145 degrees, the required safe temperature. But O'Brien came in with an attitude and expected us to virtually stop working to answer his questions. His department had the power to close a vendor down for a health code violation, as he loved to remind us.

O'Brien danced around our booth in his cream-colored sport coat and clip-on tie, feverishly jotting down notes and trying to uncover something that was amiss. He was short, with a chalkboard scratch for a voice, and he sported thick-rimmed Coke-bottle glasses. His pocket-protector was well-worn with a pair of red pens to highlight the bad stuff he could report to his supervisor. By the third time he'd lectured me on how important he was, I had had enough. I told my seventeen-year-old brother-in-law, Danny Murphy, who was working the tomato table, to slather tomato sauce over the front of his red apron and bump into O'Brien.

So, with giant, peeled pear tomato chunks clinging to his midsection, Danny gently brushed up against O'Brien and released a pleasingly plump layer of sauce, striping the back of the agent's light jacket. O'Brien was writing so fast and chirping so many warnings at us that he didn't notice. I waited a minute or so until the agent was standing alone and then barked, "Hey, O'Brien! Could you please stop dipping your sport coat into our tomato sauce!"

He followed my stare to the back of his sport coat and started screaming like a wounded beagle. He was furious, but he didn't know for sure that he hadn't done it to himself, and he couldn't conceive how we could have done it to him. He had been punked, and we laughed about it for three days.

The all-time dumbest thing we ever did also grew out of an effort at fun—an attempt to copy a certain *Saturday Night Live* skit. In our defense, we were trying to impart a touch of Lou's spirit.

When a zillion people made a beeline for pizza the moment their concert ended, we could empty our ovens in minutes, sometimes selling more than one thousand slices. Even at $1.50 a slice, that was a quick $1,500. We reloaded within seconds, like a Formula One pit stop, but there tended to be a gap of five to eight minutes when we had nothing ready to serve the people who hadn't been part of the first wave. They would hang over the counter, their eyes vacant and becoming hangrier by the moment. We'd get tired hearing, "How much longer?" So, we dreamed up some entertainment to occupy the time and keep people engaged enough to stay.

SNL had concocted a recurring sketch featuring John Belushi as a samurai in odd jobs. In at least one, he worked in a deli. That was our inspiration. We dressed Rick's roommate, Keith Ehrlich (nicknamed Psycho because his eyes bulged when he got excited), in a red skirt and sandals. He went bare chested and put his hair in a man bun. A bright yellow printed tie served as his headband. And he carried a three-foot-long steel scimitar sword that Lou had left us from his Shriner parade days when he was a member of the so-called Arab Patrol.

We debuted our show one day at Taste. As soon as we sold out and entered the pizza gap, someone stood on the prep table, demanded the attention of the waiting crowd, and introduced the Samurai Pizza Cutter. Psycho jumped out armed and in full regalia. While hundreds of people pushed and shoved to get close to our stand, Psycho grunted and talked in an unintelligible, fake Middle Eastern dialect. As soon as the crowd started chanting, "SAM-UR-EYE! SAM-UR-EYE!" at a fever pitch, Psycho brought the sword down from overhead with a roar and chopped a pizza in half. Our hungry customers went nuts!

Three times that day Psycho went through his act. Then came the fourth performance. Maybe the sword was old. Maybe the extra beers and raw meat we had fed Psycho between acts had created a little too much fervor. We will never know. But during his fourth show, when his embellishment hit a new level and the scimitar came crashing down into the unforgiving six-inch-thick butcher-block table, four inches of the steel tip snapped off and shot through the canvas roof of the tent as if it had been fired from a crossbow. It probably landed three blocks away. We never found out. But that brought the curtain down on our little entertainment, fortunately with no body count. Amen!

The festivals were throwing off profits that paid for things we needed in order to grow the business. We were sensing a little light at the end of the tunnel when my dad's old partner, George Wilson, asked us to buy him out of his 25 percent interest.

The amount he suggested we pay him was much more than the actual value of his stock. The Flossmoor failure was not yet in our rearview mirror, and we had lots of debt remaining to pay down. When we rejected his offer without a counter, he opted to sue us. In the lawsuit he filed, he accused us of taking enormous salaries and of buying multiple personal cars out of the business, neither being true. I was incensed that a guy that was supposed to be a friend of our father would stoop this low.

George sent his son, Jay, who I found to be a decent guy, to meet with me. He tried to initiate a deal, but at twenty-eight, I was stubborn and unwilling to agree to his terms. As we talked on, he asked me about how we were doing in the festivals that we entered regularly. The question caught me off guard. The festivals had become our only source of cash flow, as every bit of the income from the restaurants was going to pay our creditors. We needed that cash, and I got scared that Wilson might think that part of it was his. His next question was, "Did the profits from the festivals come back to the restaurant bank account?" Before I could answer, Jay told me that his father felt he had a right to his share of the profits from all the festivals as well.

The truth was that we had set up a separate business entity named Slavitsef, Inc. (FESTIVALS spelled backwards), out of which we ran ChicagoFest, Taste of Chicago, and all the rest of the weekend food events for which we busted our humps all summer long. We felt that it had been legitimate to run that revenue through a separate enterprise, one that Rick and I owned. Listening to Jay Wilson, I was suddenly not so sure we were right. So out of my mouth came a bold-faced lie. I told him that all the profits ran together.

Though I disagreed with his interpretation of what his dad's share should include, I didn't sleep well for two nights after I had lied to Jay Wilson. Conviction is what you feel when the judge who is seated inside your conscience declares you guilty. I felt all the associated shame that comes with conviction. I couldn't believe I had resorted to lying to someone. Who was stooping low now?

The next morning I called Wilson and confessed that I had lied to him. As embarrassed as I was to tell him, I was more relieved to get clear with my conscience. And with all the grace in the world, instead of smearing it in my face, Wilson told me he appreciated me coming clean, and he accepted my apology. By the next day we had agreed to terms on his father's buyout.

Even though it felt like a lot at the time, buying Wilson's stock meant we would own 100 percent of Malnati's. Today that equity would be worth more than three hundred times what we paid him. Giving away equity in a business you plan to grow can be dangerous!

Through this experience I had learned an important lesson as a young businessman. Frustration with another man's actions was not a reason to alter my own principles. I never wanted to have to go back to someone again and admit that I had acted without integrity. We're all going to make mistakes. But when we do, we better do the next right thing to attempt to correct the error.

8.

IN THE MIDDLE OF A sunny Sunday afternoon in August 1979, I drove to O'Hare Airport and picked up Jeanne Louise Murphy, who had been away for the summer serving as a travel camp counselor on the West Coast. Miss Murphy and I had fallen in love at the wedding of Hawk and Tina, a fraternity brother of mine and a sorority sister of hers. That memorable occasion took place over the previous Memorial Day weekend in Fort Wayne, Indiana. Jeanne left for camp a few weeks later, but we had stayed in touch via phone and that now-discarded medium, the handwritten letter. I had surprised her for a romantic lunch at Scoma's on Fisherman's Wharf during the four hours she was off duty on her camp's pit stop in San Francisco and had sweet-talked her into flying into Chicago after camp to work alongside me and our ragtag festival crew for a week before she returned home to her family in rural Illinois.

You find out a lot about a girl when you watch her work for a week without a day off. Jeanne was a star. She loved the idea of wearing whites, and she had a fantastic work ethic. Her enthusiasm and friendliness were infectious, and she was still gorgeous after sweating and splashing tomato sauce all day. She had long, straight brown hair with shimmering notes of blonde. When her hazel eyes sparkled in my direction, they turned me to

53

mush. Jeanne had grown up in Sycamore, a small farming town one and a half hours west of Chicago. She carried that sweet, small-town-America pride—a quality evident in her certainty that most everyone had heard of Sycamore (pop. eight thousand) because it was "the pumpkin capital of the world" and featured THE annual Pumpkinfest Parade.

Jeanne also had an irresistible humility. Everyone knew she was the prettiest, kindest, bring-her-home-to-mom girl on IU's campus, though she didn't seem to notice. She was clever enough to know just how to laugh to make every guy feel as if he were God's gift to comedy without quite acknowledging that she was into him. I had met her when she was a freshman little sister at our fraternity house. Getting our freshmen pledge class to invite the most attractive freshmen girls to attend little sister parties during their first few days on campus was the SAE upperclassmen's way to corral potential girlfriends without having to expend much energy. Jeanne was quickly adopted into SAE and fought over regularly.

Though she was two years behind me, Jeanne and I had been in the same giant lecture hall for a psychology class on the far end of campus. One rainy day as the class was dismissed, I asked her if she wanted a lift home. She gladly accepted, as her alternative was getting drenched. Because I knew there might never be another time I could catch Jeanne alone, and because the three-minute drive to her Delta Gamma sorority house didn't provide much chance to make an impression, I asked if she'd like to stop at Baskin-Robbins 31 Flavors for a milkshake, my treat. She gave me her sweet, "Aren't you kind!?" smile. And replied politely, "Nah. I'm good. Thanks."

WHAT??!! I wasn't asking her to go camping! The big question lurking there in the front seat of my Hugger orange Camaro: Has any guy in history ever been shut down that directly after offering a beautiful girl ice cream? Who says no to ice cream? Stunned, I pulled over at the sorority and dropped her off. Back at the fraternity, I slumped into a dark place and pondered the fact that I was a far bigger loser than I ever realized.

After that painful day, I'd see Jeanne here and there around campus or when she was hanging around at the fraternity house, but given the ice cream face-slap, I didn't risk feigning much interest. She had become the "fraternity daughter" (another term for little sister) to Scott Weiner, who had joined me at IU and SAE, and she would often visit him and his underclassmen friends.

Sometimes girls have a charming naivety and think boys are satisfied being just friends. Once, when I heard Jeanne was coming to Chicago to visit Scott, I butted in on the party and suggested that we make it a foursome and head up to the Six Flags Great America amusement park in Gurnee. Just as we were to board the park's scariest roller coaster, our dates got flip-flopped, and Weiner hopped into the snug little car with my date, and I jumped in with Jeanne. For forty-five seconds I got to laugh and scream with her as she grabbed my hand for dear life. I hoped she would give me a look or a smile or something that I could lean into to believe there might be some energy there. But nothing came of it. Once again, my hopes were dashed against the rocks by the waves of romance.

Three years later, after I'd been out of school for two years and Jeanne had just graduated, she greeted me with a hug in the receiving line of that wedding in Fort Wayne. I read some significance in her warm embrace, but with Jeanne I knew I couldn't trust my internal babe tracker. I wondered what might have changed in the two years since I'd last been rejected. Had I turned cool? Did I seem more sophisticated, now that I was a big Chicago bidnessman?

Nah. I was still the short, blond kid with the cleft lip. If there were a Facebook Live version of my life right then, my friends would be cringing, expecting to watch Marc run face first into a wall. Again. Splat.

Defying history, however, Jeanne and I separated from the pack and ended up hanging out later that night. At the after-party she had noticed I was not smoking pot, and that made her curious. I told her I was working on altering my college ways—I also told her that since the second semester of my senior year, when I joined Tom Barrett's Bible study group at the Acacia house, my faith had become important to me. I was even going to church!

Jeanne later shared her side of the story, saying it felt weird to hear me talk so openly about God in the middle of a wild party. After about twenty-five minutes, she could feel herself backing out of the conversation, yet at the same time, she felt a certain respect for my willingness to be so transparent. Amid all the music and laughter, she observed me from afar for the next hour, strangely interested. At the after-after-party at Shipwreck Jimmy's Bar in the local Holiday Inn, she and I met up again, laughing and dancing for hours. As the clock struck three in the morning and the happy crowd started to leave through the usual exits, I grabbed Jeanne's hand and whisked her through the closed hotel kitchen—making our exit through the sort of territory I knew well. As we ran through the pots and pans, Jeanne remembers thinking, "With this guy, life sure would be an adventure!"

Was it my off-center confidence that drew her in? Was she thinking that life with this guy would never be dull? Or was it that she was drawn to the spiritual search? Even she wasn't sure. But the weekend after the wedding, she rolled into Chicago to stay with her grandmother while she ostensibly visited Scott. She and he had remained friends but not of a serious romantic nature. Because he had to work during the day, I delightfully volunteered to be her daylight tour guide since I was working nights at the pizzerias.

That first day we hiked through Harms Woods, a popular forest preserve on the North Shore. Jeanne had been an outdoor recreation major; she loved nature, and I did, too. We walked and talked in the company of giant oaks and their saplings. Spring was giving way to summer, so the foliage was bursting. For a few hours, we shared our lives while I silently prayed that I'd never wake from this dream. We came to an old tree with low-hanging branches and decided to climb it. Moments later, we found ourselves standing on a narrow perch about fifteen feet above the forest floor, with our faces only twelve inches apart. As I looked at her and her eyes sparkled back at me, the light hit her face in a magical way—the same way it lit Glenn Close in *The Natural* as she stood in the grandstand, an orchestra playing music in her head, and watched Robert Redford hit a long home run. In that unforgettable moment I kissed Jeanne, and she didn't resist. Of course, she was trapped there with me on the tree branch, but she seemed to like it.

Scott brought Jeanne into the restaurant later that night, and when she walked into the bar, I whispered to one of the regulars, "I'm gonna marry that girl." The next day, a Saturday, turned into one of those synchronicity experiences that defy worldly explanation. A few months before, I had thrown my name into the contest bucket at a prominent record store, and that Saturday the store notified me that I had won the grand prize—a diamond (the contest was promoting a group called The Diamonds). So, I took Jeanne with me into the city to the three-year-old Water Tower Place mall on Michigan Avenue, and together we collected my prize at a jewelry store. When we walked out, we both silently felt a bolt of energy or a shared insight—we were carrying the diamond that would soon find itself perched upon the ring finger of her left hand.

I still can't recall that weekend without goose bumps. We'll always remember that trip into the city, but, more than that, we'll remember the moment in the tree when time stopped, and we both recognized that we wanted to be together forever. I was certain that God had connected us in a magical way.

Jeanne had planned to move to Estes Park, Colorado, where she had worked as a wrangler for high school girls at Cheley Camps, but instead, we had fallen in love. The following month, we were engaged. My mom served us champagne with sliced peaches every day for a week. I could only imagine how Lou would have been, spoiling his first daughter. We met Jeanne's parents, Ron and Bev, for dinner, and they asked us to wait at least a year since we had just begun dating.

Five months later, we were married.

9.

OUR FIRST YEAR OF MARRIAGE was rough. We had bought a new little house in Wilmette, but I was running the night shift in Lincolnwood, closing the store down five or six times each week. I would get home around two in the morning, still wound up and ready to listen to some music and have something to eat. Jeanne had taken a job with the Skokie Park District, creating programming for kids and seniors, and she worked nine to five Monday through Friday.

Clearly, our schedules didn't jibe. I had recreated Lou World because I could hear his gravelly voice in my head: "You've got to be there on the weekends. That's when your bread gets buttered. Wednesdays and Thursdays are a little tricky. We're running a weekday schedule, but sometimes we get busy just cuz, so you want to be around to make it go with that shorter crew. You always want to stop in on Monday to make sure the ordering for the week is right, so you don't get caught with your pants down. Take Tuesdays if you need a day off." He spoke his gospel in a matter-of-fact way, instructions that I would immediately download as my operating system. One of my biggest challenges would be to still his voice so that I could discover a different way to manage the restaurants, or as Sinatra sang, "my way."

Jeanne thought I was ridiculous. Her dad had been an executive at Ideal Industries, and he worked seven to five four days a week. They lived two minutes from his office, so he was home for lunch every day and for cocktails before family dinners every night by 5:02 p.m. They had three-day weekends to go up to Madison for Wisconsin football games, and he never missed a family party or a wedding. Work on holidays? Never.

We were only about six months into marital bliss when, in the middle of our first real fight about my schedule, the "D" word leaked out. I couldn't blame Jeanne. I had already lived through this movie, and it was not pretty. Even if my parents' marriage had been better, Lou's work hours would have been a problem. That and Dewar's White Label. Something had to change, and it didn't take a genius to see that it was up to me. How would I put family first and still run a restaurant business?

I was sitting slumped on our front steps one Tuesday when Jeanne came home from work. I had spent a few hours that day at the French antique store down the block. The owner was a master carpenter who had learned the trade from his father. He devoted his days to running the shop and restoring tongue-and-groove drawers and refinishing armoires that had been built centuries earlier. He loved that I was interested, and he spent time explaining the multiple painstaking steps each repair required. I thought about my great-grandfather Ernesto Malnati, Adolfo's dad, an expert sculptor who had come from Italy and lived in Vermont. Maybe I carried some artisan DNA. When Jeanne sat down on the stoop to comfort me, I told her that I was thinking that maybe I should abandon the restaurant business and learn to be a carpenter from my new friend, Jacques.

I loved many things about the restaurant business. I'm a doer. An achiever. An Enneagram 3. I'm addicted to busyness. Scratching things off my list jacks me up. If I accomplish, I have value. When I don't, I have none. That made the restaurant business a perfect fit for an adrenaline junkie like me. But I couldn't imagine a future when I wouldn't be working nights on the floor and managing the actions and characters in a bar.

I'd been doing that for the past two years at Lincolnwood after doing it in Flossmoor. Being away from Jeanne and our eventual family most nights would produce a decent salary, but my greatest fear was that I would become Lou, the phantom husband and father—that I'd live amid a bar culture and miss out on everything but AA.

The carpenter idea remained for about a week. I admired the work, but I didn't feel joy when I sat with it. Getting out of town was the perfect segue, and Jeanne and I jumped at the opportunity to travel to Newcastle, England, to consult with a large British brewery that wanted to introduce Chicago pan pizza into some of their pubs. The challenge of recreating the fun and friendliness of Malnati's, the trials of replicating the product in another country, and the raw energy I felt in starting something ground up shifted me into that "genuinely gratifying state of consciousness" that Mihaly Csikszentmihalyi, the great Hungarian-born psychologist who taught at the University of Chicago, speaks of in his classic book, *Flow*.

In Newcastle I learned that our dough would require local adjustments based on water and climate. I had brought one of my best kitchen operatives, Marc Miller, an eighteen-year-old kid who would run through walls for me. Between us, we transformed the raw materials available in England into a pizza of which we could be proud. Jeanne aided with the hiring and training of the front of the house staff and helped them adopt the American brand of friendliness. We had a riot collecting all sorts of Chicago memorabilia to adorn the walls—street signs, posters, vintage newspapers, campaign buttons, you name it!

In the end, our partners had not chosen a solid site for operating, and our store only lasted a few years. But the joy of opening that restaurant infused me with energy. It restored my confidence and reconfirmed my love for the restaurant business. And while we were in England, I dreamed up the concept of a carryout shoppe, which turned out to be a pretty good idea.

We would build little kitchens where we would make the same great pizza but without the hassle of running a dining room or a bar. Carryout had always been a key factor in our revenue, and if we ran the operation tight, this might be a model for expansion. I had been looking for a way to divorce myself from the liquor part of the business, and that divorce was far preferable to one from my new bride. Maybe this was a way we could grow our business, albeit in a different way than Lou had envisioned.

We opened our first carryout store—1,100 square feet—in a strip mall in Wilmette in 1981 and then another in Northbrook in 1982, right around the time our first daughter, Kelsey, was born. For decor, we wanted to speak to tradition and heritage, so we went to school on a hundred-year-old photo of Barbara Noll, my sweet grandma, and her mother. In the picture, they were standing in the little corner grocery they owned in Chicago. Jeanne (and our baby daughter) helped me decorate the customer areas of the new stores with vintage tin food cans and turn-of-the-century wooden kitchen tools. The bright orange signs announced "Lou Malnati's Pasta & Pizza"—which turned out to be a mistake.

We imagined that adding fresh pasta to the mix might bolster sales. Why not give it a shot? Here's why it turned out to be a bad idea: When you try something new, add it as a limited-time offer to see if it gains traction. Don't use it as a headliner. I've noticed in the years since that when a pizzeria suddenly advertises "Fish Fry Friday," you can be assured that you're witnessing that restaurant's death rattle. If you're a pizzeria, you better be able to make bank on your pizza or you will soon be looking for another career.

We bought fancy pasta machines and beautiful four-color pasta boxes and buckets. And we never sold any pasta. We changed the signs as fast as we could. To this day, I keep one of our never-used, four-color "fresh spaghetti" boxes on the mantle in my office just to remind me to focus on what we do better than everyone else. Know your niche, Mitch.

I feel the same way about knowing where and how to sell our pizza. We are often courted by major league sports franchises, such as the Cubs and the Bulls, eager to sell Malnati's pizza in their venues. But after the team and their concessionaires take their markup, the pizza would sell for $8.50 a slice. And while it would be delicious before the game when it's freshly baked and when most fans are buying food, it would be difficult to maintain our high standards as the game went on. In the middle of the second half, after the pizzas have been sitting for too long, we'd end up charging a customer $8.50 for a lukewarm, not-so-flaky slice. Do you think there's any chance that customer will bring their family into our restaurant the following week? A stadium presence might sound good on paper, but you only last fifty years by staying in your lane. Important lesson there.

The carryout pasta lasted only a few months. After that, we sold only pizza, salad, and soda. The best part about the new stores was their schedule—open only from 4:00 p.m. to 10:00 p.m. six days a week. We could easily run one with two managers. What wasn't so great was that they weren't doing much volume. We weren't losing money, but we weren't getting rich by a long shot.

Would our plan to open fifty of these and never have to deal again with Lou's bar customers go up in smoke? What were we missing?

Of course, we tried other concepts. We ventured into opening a pizza-by-the-slice operation downtown. But that idea ran into the same problem our pizza would have faced at a stadium venue: The pizza was great when we had volume but not very good when we didn't. We opened an Italian ice store in Little Italy, but then we remembered that Chicago features eight months of winter. We tried lots of things that garnered C+ results.

Still, I'd picked up the desire to expand from my dad. Lou wanted to be Ray Kroc. I wasn't that far gone, but I loved the idea of growing the Malnati's pizza legacy. We served great food, and I wanted more people to enjoy it. I wanted the company to have a larger footprint, and I wanted to increase opportunities for the folks who worked for us. Plus, I loved the hunt—the search for a new location, pulling together the elements to open a new restaurant.

So, we kept trying, and one of the reasons we were more creative and entrepreneurial was that a new, key member had joined our team full time: my brother, Rick.

Rick had attended Bradley University on a Division I basketball scholarship. He was a gifted athlete, always the best in his class through high school. Scott Weiner and I joked that we had toughened him up on our front yard court when he was little. Rick was four years younger, but he could use his quickness to get around any of us for an easy layup, even knowing that as soon as he left his feet, he would likely get shoved through the five-foot wall of evergreen bushes planted under the basket.

As a high school senior, Rick took New Trier West to the school's first downstate appearance in the state basketball tournament. That led to his recruitment to Bradley as a point guard, where he was sixth man on an NCAA tournament team that featured two guys who made it to the NBA. At six feet tall, he was a scrappy defender and a fiery floor leader who made his teammates better. When Bradley played Indiana State, Rick guarded Larry Bird for much of the game. He jokes that he held Bird to forty-six points, but the truth was that he could shut down just about anyone, including Bird.

Rick probably wouldn't have chosen the restaurant business. He was basically living the dream of being an adored college athlete, when college up and ended with his graduation. He wasn't IBM material since he had pretty much hated the school part of school. But he liked having money in his pocket. Finding himself without a lot of options, he picked up his pizza clamps and became my partner.

Rick will work without stopping and maintain a pace that few would consider. He is fueled by equal portions aggression and passion. The latent insecurity that we Malnati brothers carry often shows up in a fiercely competitive way—the need to prove that we can kick your ass. My manner is sneakier, while Rick's is more overt. He would show you that he could make pizzas quicker, match them with order tickets more efficiently, and handle the constant burns while screaming at you and everyone else to go faster. He possessed a mastery of the English language, in a dark web sort of way, a skill that had been passed down directly from Lou and would keep the whole staff highly entertained. (Most of the words are too colorful to repeat here.) God forbid, he caught you making a mistake that you wouldn't admit, as he would love to bring it up for a public debate.

Rick opened the stand at ChicagoFest one morning in the early 1980s. As he fired the ovens up for the day, he discovered twelve totally charred pizzas that someone had failed to remove and sell at the end of the previous night. He did his research and determined that nineteen-year-old Ronnie Caras, a great kid and a hard worker, had been the closing ovenman. Instead of throwing the pizzas out, Rick preserved them in the oven until three that afternoon when poor Ronnie returned to work. Before he had his apron tied, Rick asked, "Hey, Ronnie, will you check that top oven for me?"

Ronnie flipped open the door and beheld the dozen black pizzas. "We've got a new name for you, Ronnie," Rick told him. "It's Scorch." When Ronnie started to plead his case, Rick was ready. "Oh! It wasn't you? Who was the last guy working the ovens last night? Oh! Maybe someone snuck into the stand in the middle of the night and burnt them? No! It couldn't have been you, Scorchy Boy!" He went on and on until he had helped this kid learn that being defensive after making a mistake was the worst sin imaginable.

Recently, after not seeing Ronnie for thirty years, I ran into him at the golf course. The first thing he said was, "Marc, I swear I didn't burn those pizzas!" He told me with a smile that some of his friends still call him Scorch. What had been an embarrassing lesson had created a cherished place for Ronnie in the Malnati festival lore. As Ronnie made peace with the error, he had cemented himself as an integral part of Rick's team. He had been seen by Rick, and Rick was larger than life in the eyes of a college kid.

The dynamic was the same in our stores. Rick's humor, which could be used as a weapon, shot rubber bullets. While he kept the world slightly off-balance with his barbs, he embedded himself in people's hearts by loving them and by really seeing them. He carried a fat wad of cash, just as Lou had taught us, and he was a soft touch for a server or a cook who had hit a rough patch. He made it his business to find good, cheap used cars, often parking two or three in his driveway, because he knew there were people on our team who would need them.

For years, Rick fought like crazy with our mother's second husband, Richard Miller. Rick and Dick shared the same birthday and the same temperament. They competed regularly to see who could be the most stubborn. But later in life, when Dick began to lose his ability to walk and when dementia started setting in, Rick was the one regularly taking my mom to visit him, making sure he was being cared for and bringing him his favorite root beer and strawberry milkshakes. Rick was generous to a fault, and you could depend on him showing up when you were struggling, no matter what had transpired in the past.

Maybe that's why our mom doted on him and gave him all her attention. Maybe it was because he'd be the first one to respond to her calls. The favoritism did seem to start when we were young, though. I'm not certain because my memory is not all that good—certainly not as good as Jeanne's, who remembers which outfit she wore to a party twenty-two years ago. At the same time, I'm not opposed to embellishment—that is, massaging the details of a vaguely remembered story until the tale gets to a place where most people hearing it will laugh hard enough to spit out their drink.

Which brings me to the time when I was six years old and Rick was two, and we were grocery shopping with my mom. She let me push the cart. I think she walked over to grab some apples or guacamoles or something and was feeling them to see if they were too squishy. I was bored watching her, so I kept moving, and when she eventually caught up to me with her satchel of fruit, she asked where the cart was. Upon examination, she discovered that it had been abandoned in the corner of the meat department. She was really upset with me, and after that she never let me push the cart again when my little two-year-old brother was in it. I guess because he was crying like he always did, she was embarrassed when she found him alone next to the salmon. I might have earned a spanking. I'm not sure, because, as I said, my memory is not great, and that's a piece of the story I would have embellished right out.

Even though he was the reason I got into lots of trouble when we were young, Rick and I merged and created a formidable partnership. And after some of the ideas for expanding our brand without alcohol didn't pay off as well as we would have liked, we knew we needed another plan if we were to grow our fledgling business. That required me to come to grips with the prospect of opening full-service restaurants. Fortunately, America's habits—and liquor laws—were changing by the mid-eighties. Mothers Against Drunk Driving (MADD) and other groups had created a movement against one of America's ills. As drinkers began to lose their licenses and serve jail time, spending long shifts at local watering holes was a far less attractive option. Increasingly, the bars at our restaurants became waiting areas for people coming for dinner. They might enjoy a beverage, but they weren't on the path to ruining their family's life by spending six to eight hours on their proprietary stool, as had been the case at Lou's in Lincolnwood in the 1970s.

Meantime, as we expanded the business, my hours improved because I had to be around during the day. That's when the planning for and opening of new restaurants took place. No more harried late nights, a relief for me and for my family, and a marked departure from the way my dad said it needed to be done.

Without Lou's presence as the resident personality, Lincolnwood lost its biggest draw, and the regulars slowly moved or passed away. My mom did her best to host when she was around, but she had found a partner in Richard, who loved to travel and attend sporting events with her. He also owned a car dealership and a home near Peoria, so she spent time there.

It was about then that I asked Mom to sell the company to Rick and me for an amount that would ensure her a steady income for the rest of her life, enough that she would never need to be dependent on anyone else.

Jeanne and I had been attending church regularly, and at this juncture in my life, I had begun to pray more. Though I didn't feel that I got a clear message back, I sensed that this business was where God had placed me. Since He wasn't creating any other options that I was aware of, I finally decided it was fine, even good, that I would stay in it and do my best with the opportunity. Mom agreed to sell the business to Rick and me, and we signed the papers.

10.

LOOKING BACK, MY EXPERIENCE HAS taught me one fundamental rule of business: If you want to build a thriving company, surround yourself with outstanding people.

Peachy Lis was the general manager of our Elk Grove restaurant, and her husband, Eddie, presided over the buying for all the stores. He also managed the floor on weekend nights and visited restaurants in the early morning. Peachy and Eddie had formed the bridge that kept Malnati's operating while Lou fought cancer, and while my brother and I grew into our leadership roles. Peachy and Eddie had no children other than Rick and me, effectively their adopted sons, and they did absolutely everything in their power to ensure our success.

Peachy was a lifelong veteran of the restaurant business and had worked alongside Lou for twenty-two years downtown at Pizzeria Due. Lou evoked loyalty from people because they knew he would be ready and willing to help them if they were in trouble. He had been there for her when she fought her way through a battle with alcohol, and she never forgot it. She came with Lou to open Lincolnwood, and Ed sold his business in 1975 and followed her. They were committed to great food, to doing things the right way, and, most importantly, they were committed to Rick and me. When our daughter Kelsey was born, she was not only the first Malnati grandchild, but Peachy and Ed celebrated her as their first grandchild as well. Peachy built a giant candy castle in Elk Grove as part of her Christmas decorations and named it Kelsey's Kastle. She named a special drink after her and insisted all her guests try it.

Peachy made all kids feel as if they were the most special little people in the world, and she always treated them with unwavering respect. She stood Rick on a milk crate and taught him how to work the cash register when he was eleven! Each year she and her lead server, Vicki Lucki, would create a Christmas pageant with full costumes and props, starring all the teenagers who worked in the store. They made a giant, hollowed-out snowman out of Styrofoam packing peanuts. Vicki would sneak inside him, and Frosty would dance and lead carols for all the customers in the restaurant to sing together. Peachy and Vicki suggested having our first company picnic in Busse Woods, an event that grew pre-COVID-19 to welcome over three thousand people.

Eddie worked out of the shoebox office we had above the Lincolnwood restaurant. He had little formal education, but he was great with numbers. He had hustled his entire life, working in a liquor store as a kid and eventually owning his own pawnshop. He created predictive systems for ordering product from our vendors that were way ahead of Apple, including a way to track the expected depletion of cheese, sausage, tomatoes, and such based on every thousand dollars of sales. He'd routinely call our restaurants and say, "You either miscounted your pepperoni or you better start looking for a thief." As a buyer, he would give off that little smirky smile to keep a vendor off-balance, not sure if Ed liked him or not. When Ed thought a vendor wasn't giving us what he called "a fair shake," he'd get out his red pen and adjust the invoice lower, and that's what we would pay. He would repeat it again and again until he finally got the vendor to relent and adjust our pricing to what he had determined was fair.

Eddie and Peachy liked to gamble, and they'd religiously go to Vegas for two long weekends a year. But that would be their only time away from the business because they loved work more than they liked vacations. Ed would start his days at 4:30 a.m., seven days a week, stopping at each restaurant to count out the safe and make sure deposits had been made the night before. He'd take a quick inventory to double-check the manager's count and to make sure we had enough product to get through the night or the weekend. On his way out, he'd walk through the kitchen checking for cleanliness. Once he made it into his office, he'd deal with any of the issues he'd turned up during his early morning patrol and promptly begin beating up the vendors. He did that every single day, like a Swiss watch. The vendors used to grumble that he was an SOB, but a fair SOB.

Serving people lit Peachy up. She loved to get in early and cook the lunch specials herself, taking suggestions from her loyal band of regular guests who responded to her effusive brand of hospitality. As New York restaurateur Danny Meyer says, "People always felt she was on their side." She knew everyone's name, and nobody was a stranger in her store. She fostered that welcoming spirit among all her staff, because she had learned over many years that the team around her would make or break the restaurant. She had a waitstaff that embraced her customers as if they were family, and a kitchen crew she could always depend on.

Peachy was at the front door to welcome you, and even if she needed to sprint, she was there again to thank you when you were on your way out. She had patience with others and their quirks, and she catered to people's special needs. If you wanted your soup sitting on the table when you walked in, she would have it there. Specific booth or table? She'd remember. If you were forty-two but still preferred to sit on a booster seat, she had you covered.

Peachy and I discovered the property that would become our Schaumburg restaurant while out on a scouting tour in early 1985. It stood on the corner of Roselle and Schaumburg roads, which had been Main

& Main during the 1800s when German settlers fashioned a small town thirty miles northwest of Chicago. The place was called the Schaumrose Inn, and we had lunch in a booth in the bar, where old pictures detailed some of the inn's history. Back in the days of dirt roads and horse-and-buggy transportation, the little restaurant had been a neighborhood hub along with Old St. Peter's Church across the street, which was established in 1847. A plan to redevelop this area as the Olde Schaumburg Centre had recently been embraced by the village fathers.

After five hard years, we had finally paid off the entire debt from the failure of our Flossmoor store, and we were in position to grow. We had developed a good name in the area due to thirteen years of Peachy's leadership in nearby Elk Grove.

The Schaumrose Inn's owner, Vic Binneboese, was our server that bright winter afternoon when Peachy and I lunched there. Vic told us that he and his brother-in-law, Wayne Nebel, had run the restaurant forever, and they had planned to retire and become landlords to a new operator. But the guy who had assumed the reins had nearly run the place into the ground over the past two years, and they had unhappily returned to active service when his rent checks started bouncing. The income was critical to both in their retirement, and they had had no choice but to get out of their rocking chairs and put their aprons back on. Clearly, they wanted out.

Vic showed us the second floor of the property, which was not currently being used. The space was divided into small bedrooms where long-ago travelers to and from Chicago might have bunked down on their way back and forth to the West. He whispered a rumor that the Inn had been a rent-a-room-by-the-hour kind of place in the 1930s for the likes of Al Capone and his contemporaries. Peachy and I could clearly imagine pulling these walls down to unpack a large dining room with a grand staircase in the center. The frame building had a "Victorian meets Eastern seaboard" look to it, with a widow's walk above the roof. It had an inviting curbside appeal, and we imagined painting it in four colors in the painted lady style that would enhance the architectural details. We believed we could increase the seating from thirty to 150 and really have a chance to do some business. We left very excited.

We struck a great deal with Vic and Wayne to buy the property with a small, $20,000 down payment, and they agreed to hold the mortgage and serve as our quasi-bank. In a preliminary conversation with the village, we began to realize that we were in the right place at the right time. A little wink from God. The village had evidently been looking for a while for the perfect family restaurant to complete their Olde Schaumburg Centre development. When we came along, the members of the village board opened their arms and allowed us to move with relative ease through what typically can be a tedious and lengthy process of town meetings. We engaged a contractor and opened the doors in October 1985. Peachy pruned her Elk Grove staff, sending Jeannie Anderson to be GM and bringing experienced staff from both the kitchen and the dining room, assignments that created solid leadership at the new store.

Fortunately, Schaumburg was an immediate success, though there was a lot of angst leading up to the opening date, as construction extras piled up, and we needed robust sales to pay for them. Four profitable years later, we were in position to go back to Vic and Wayne and consummate the sale of the restaurant, the two-story office building across the parking lot, and two barns that were home to small businesses, all for $300,000, a price that sounds crazy low as I write it today.

About three months before we opened Schaumburg, we convinced Stu Cohen to leave his accounting firm and become our partner at Malnati's. We imagined Stu being a steadying financial presence, but he proved to be so much more. In his first six months, he saved us more than double his salary by renegotiating what we were paying for professional services, such as insurance, banking, and accounting. He instituted regularity in our store meetings to review the numbers, and he taught our store managers how to read their profit and loss statements. He wanted to make everyone around him a better businessman or businesswoman, and he did it with a warmth that never made anyone feel stupid. He was never too busy to work with someone to brainstorm an issue or even to listen to a personal challenge they might be dealing with. He cared about people and loved to see them learn and grow. He was far gentler than Rick or me, so people would seek him out for his coaching before they'd ever bring an issue to us.

Stu was humble and self-deprecating about areas in which he either had no skill or had no intention to gain any, such as anything technical—programming his phone or changing the paper on his printer. Or anything that had to do with cooking or cleaning. He was always willing to lend his support via "atta-boys," but he knew his limitations. Back surgery in his early 30s scarred him physically. The operation caused just enough paranoia for him to start believing he might never walk again. A solid athlete in his youth, he stopped participating for several years in most every athletic endeavor or activity that would require much standing. He gained more weight than he wanted to, and though he was always self-conscious about being heavy, he was always willing to talk about it. There was no guile, no pretense with Stu. He was loved universally at Malnati's, like a big teddy bear.

Stu would ride through potential neighborhoods on Sundays for hours on end, often accompanied by his wife, Gerri, counting rooftops and scouting new sites for our stores. Yes, he was the guy on top of our numbers, but not in a geeky, tightfisted accountant sort of way. He created tight budgets but realized that while it was important to guard expenses, the thing that would help us most to grow our earnings was building sales. Yes, he was a CPA, but he also had an MBA in marketing from the University of Illinois, and he was a rabid marketer.

He believed, like us, that getting our pizza into people's mouths was our truest mission—after that, everything would begin to take care of itself. He loved to work with local schools to build programs with kids. Stu was convinced that if we could get kids to adopt our product at an early age, we'd have them for life. Not a bad model to build around.

Stu talked me into engaging Christie Fowler, a real estate consultant from his old firm. He knew that we must not repeat our grievous mistake in Flossmoor. Christie taught us the critical factors to measure and take into consideration before deciding on a restaurant location. She took data from our existing stores to show how far our customers were driving to eat our pizza. Knowing that helped us know what we might expect in subsequent neighborhoods. We could draw about a five-mile circle around our suburban restaurants (less than half that size in the city because of density) and that circle contained about 90 percent of our guests. Our gut might have told us the same thing, but Christie showed us the importance of backing up our instincts with data.

We made a study of the demographics of the inhabitants of our current markets, especially marking income levels and the density of homes. Our proximity to homes was important for dine-in, but especially critical to our carryout and delivery business, and for a suburban pizzeria to be successful, it needed to crush all three components. One of the best lessons was that expressways or village borders often create artificial boundaries to neighborhoods where people like to shop or dine, and those boundaries can bisect your circle and impede your revenue potential. We looked at how many cars passed a location daily and asked if the parking was substantial or if we would have to depend on neighbors' lots. Was it easy to enter our lot or was the ingress/egress confusing? Would the village allow for proper signage? Where was the competition located, and what were they doing well? Learning to be more astute at choosing locations early on in our growth made a real difference and gave us far better odds for success and a real competitive advantage.

Stu helped with researching new locations and then supervised the leasing and anything else that required a contract. He willingly immersed himself in the legal details to protect the company, a chore for which I clearly didn't have the patience. He brought uniformity to everything that I ran by the seat of my pants. Any part of the business in which he inserted himself benefited from the structure he would apply, and he got into almost everything. He wanted to see our people paid well, so he supervised payroll and our bonus program for managers. Stu would soon be granted the title of president because there were few details that escaped him. He was a critical part of building a foundation for future growth, and after a few more key hires, we were able to seek out deals for restaurants in River North and Buffalo Grove in those next few years. And that period would be the scariest course-changing era in the life of Malnati's.

11.

TEN MONTHS AFTER OPENING SCHAUMBURG and now fifteen years after Lincolnwood, we opened our first downtown restaurant in Chicago's River North. The River North of the 1980s was just beginning to shake off its reputation as a skid row. After Jimmy DeRose asked our mutual friend Jack Weiner for an introduction, DeRose approached us about putting our next store into the first floor of his small office building on Wells and Hubbard. He knew that the only way he could get us to consider this area would be to promise to kiss us into the deal. In other words, he would bear all the expenses to get the restaurant ready for operation, and we would step in and operate it. Jimmy was an astute real estate investor and developer, and he believed deeply in the potential of the neighborhood. After he spent some time walking us through it, we were convinced as well.

Opening two restaurants in two years resulted in promotions all around the company. We had plenty of capable people and were now challenging them with bigger responsibilities. In addition to bringing Stu into the front office, we brought in a Culinary Institute of America trained chef named Jim Freeland to build efficiency and consistency into all our kitchens. He professionalized our systems and tried to teach our

people the best way to perform their roles. But change was not read-
ily accepted by everyone. People who had started at Malnati's with Lou
fifteen years earlier didn't necessarily fancy the idea of new, and often
younger, bosses. Why would we fix something that wasn't broken?
Peachy grumbled, "Who was the guy walking into my kitchen and telling
our cooks that they weren't following the recipe when they were making
meat sauce and minestrone soup?"

We were in a growth spurt, our people were working without
taking days off, and petty frustrations were at an all-time high. Our
culture was fast becoming one characterized by gossip, sarcasm, and
backstabbing. I felt it, and knew we'd have to deal with it. But just then,
life happened at home. Slightly over a year before, our second child, a
boy, had been born. We named him Will, after Willie Noll, my mater-
nal grandfather, who had died months before the baby's birth. At nine
months, he began throwing up almost every day. At eleven months,
Jeanne's mom babysat for him and voiced her concern. We were bringing him to see our pediatrician almost every other week. His assurance
that Will would grow out of it when he began to walk sort of lulled us
to sleep. But by the time Will was fourteen months old, Jeanne and I
weren't seeing big improvement. He wasn't gaining weight, and he still
wasn't strong enough to walk; his head drooped to the side and seemed
too heavy for his tiny neck to support. We brought him to Children's
Memorial Hospital (now Lurie Children's Hospital) for tests. Jeanne
slept at the hospital for two weeks straight as the specialists tried to
determine what was wrong.

There can't be many things in life more terrifying than imagining
that your infant child could be really sick. The doctors ran tests and
more tests. Eventually, they determined that the sphincter muscle leading to his stomach had failed to develop. Given his age, when it became
clear that surgery was the only option, the doctors weren't sure he would
survive. Our family, our friends, and our entire church prayed for Willie.
God was merciful, bringing him out the other side. We fed him formula

through a tube that stuck out of his stomach for months following, as he healed and began gaining weight.

During this ordeal, Jeanne never left Willie's side and nursed him back to health. I would visit the hospital every day, try to keep things going at work, and spend the evening and night with our daughter, Kelsey, then four. Rich Blue (the guy who took the brass knuckles to his head) had gone on to become a Christian therapist in private practice. He and his wife, Sue, had a daughter just a few months older than Kelsey, and they offered to have Kelsey stay at their home. I would stop in at their house after work. During one of those late evenings, Rich and I got to talking about the state of affairs at Malnati's. I confided that we were struggling culturally, and that our people, like most people, had no idea how to resolve conflict. I told him that dealing with the drama was more than I could handle. Given that his ideals aligned with mine and that he had consulted for other businesses, I asked him if he would be willing to do a one-day training for our top leaders and share tools we could use to right our ship.

Jeanne and I had joined an Adult Children of Alcoholics (ACOA) therapy group—her father, like mine, had had a drinking problem—and we were learning about dealing with the conflict that was always present in dysfunctional families, such as the families in which we had both grown up. Families like ours were steeped in secrets and codependency and caught in a repetitive pattern of avoiding issues. Codependency was one of the big words of the day, as Melody Beattie's book, *Codependent No More*, debuted in 1986. Beattie believed that people who lived with addicts could lose themselves in the drama of a family member's destructive behavior. She taught people how to stop trying to control the uncontrollable and to learn to take care of themselves first. In the ACOA group that Jeanne and I joined, we were learning ways to communicate that had not been taught in school and had certainly not been taught at home. We were learning the importance of identifying what we really wanted and then asking for it, versus blaming others for our unhappiness. Could what we were learning and experiencing in therapy be translated into skills that would work in business?

Rich agreed to help us, and our first meeting was in a conference room down the street from our restaurant in Lincolnwood. We met at the old purple Hyatt House Hotel, the place where just a few years prior, mob frontman Allen Dorfman was gunned down before he could testify against the Chicago syndicate. We set aside four hours on a Monday, and Rick and I and our ten top leaders sat with Rich in a circle. There were no conference tables to hide behind, and no pens or paper to divert our attention. The ground rules were that Rich would teach and moderate the session, and everyone would have an equal voice. The voices of Rick and me would be no more important than anyone else's. Titles were to be checked at the door. We planned to learn key tools around sharing and then to work on giving honest feedback and resolving conflict. We assumed that four hours would give us more than enough time to clear out the relational cobwebs that seemed to be slowing down our team. We knew we had some issues, but I truly believed that four hours would suffice.

We all sat looking at each other, smiling sheepishly, like school kids summoned to the principal's office. I was excited with the possibilities for the meeting, but my truest feeling was fear. Would this work? Would the people on the team buy in? Would they be willing to be vulnerable? Would they think I was out of my mind to inflict this on them?

It turned out that identifying feelings and expressing them became a critical, life-giving exercise in all our lives. We learned the acronym SASHET: Sad, Angry, Scared, Happy, Excited, and Tender. This created a simple language that distilled the hundreds of words we use to describe feelings into six bite-size chunks. We would take turns sharing what we were feeling, which was far more transparent and interesting than hearing whether the Cubs won or lost or what kind of weather was coming our way. Instead, we established a new level of vulnerability that created a tangible intimacy. That helped me know my colleagues better and, just as important, helped me know myself better. And people weren't pushed away by the authentic me, even when I was angry. They actually trusted me more.

That first meeting at the purple Hyatt started slowly, but it didn't take long until all hell broke loose. Finger pointing and pent-up frustrations. Shaming. It all bubbled up to the surface. Peachy told Jim Freeland, our new chef, that his ideas were going to screw up the kitchen and ruin the business. Several team members complained that another team member always cried when she was questioned. And she cried. On and on. We unpacked stories we had made up about each other. But Rich taught us to check out those stories to see how much was fact and how much was fiction. Rich gave us a model for clearing the air of our judgments and frustrations with each other. That meant meticulously walking through those judgments with the person who was frustrating us and doing it in front of the entire group. At the end of four hours, we were exhausted, but felt we had made progress and decided that four weeks later, we would assemble the same group and finish up.

That next month came, and as soon as butts hit the chairs, we were off to the races, working through the reservoir of issues that was deeper than anyone realized. We gained ground but knew there was more that had to come out. So, we did it again. And again . . . and again!

For at least a year we had no idea that we were launching a bigger idea, a way to create strong connections and a family-like business dynamic—a far healthier dynamic than most of us had experienced growing up or in any workplace setting. This concept of meeting took on the simple name Group and would later be reframed as Compass Group, a place that could point you in the right direction. We would share our lives and share the emotions that we had previously protected as private, a practice that initially seemed almost unthinkable. Sometimes we would even venture into personal, family matters outside the business. We opened up about the things that made us angry, the things that scared us to death, the things that made us cry . . . the things that made us human. Making a conscious choice to reveal and be known at that level, and to feel trust and to be trusted, was like superglue for those of us who drank the Kool-Aid.

Being in Group was an invitation to walk down the road to self-awareness. We quickly realized that there is no end to that road. And it promises to take us through frustrating curves and up and down steep hills, sometimes into oncoming traffic. The challenge for me became learning about myself and being open to making changes in my leadership style based on feedback I received. We learned that holding a mirror up for one of our colleagues to see their blind spots was one of the greatest gifts we could give. Embracing your dark side can be frightening, but living it together and supporting each other to become the best leaders we were capable of becoming was worth the price of admission.

We held openness and transparency as the bar, and Rich taught us to clean things up with each other when we realized we were holding back or starting to build a protective wall between us and one of our colleagues. We instituted the 24-Hour Rule, which dictated that if we said something critical about another person, we had twenty-four hours to share it directly with that person. As time went on, we learned about diffusing conflict before we started arming our nuclear weapons. We learned to release our "story" about a conflict and became willing to listen to the other person describe their version. We learned to supportively and constructively coach ane another when we noticed a trait or habit or attitude that really got under our skin. Ultimately, we realized that the things that made us mad or drove us crazy about others were the things that offered the most valuable lessons about ourselves. Psychology calls that *projection*. As the AA *Big Book* says, "You spot it, you got it!"

Group expanded as Malnati's grew. We added a second circle of our top leaders after about three years. Later, our own leaders would work in pairs to serve as facilitators for new groups as we sought to include all our managers and directors. By 2010, we were hosting upwards of twenty groups. Participation wasn't mandatory, and there were a few team members who chose to opt out, but 95 percent of our people recognized the benefit of the lessons that Group could provide, not just at Malnati's, but in their families as well. Though there are hundreds of people who have let their thoughts be known over the years, here are a couple of my favorite comments (with names and titles changed for privacy):

• "I've benefited most in my personal life. I came home and began to share feelings with my wife. I believe our marriage was saved because I was able to more vulnerably communicate my fear and sadness, and to truly hear her." —Alan, General Manager

• "Because of what I learned and experienced in Group, I told my dad that I loved him for the first time, while he was in the hospital on his deathbed." —Theresa, Catering Director

• "I thought my new manager hated me. But I took the risk of sharing my fear and checked it out with him. It led to us understanding one another and getting along so much better. In my old job, I would've held onto my mistaken belief forever." —Jennifer, Server

Rich was the perfect leader for these meetings. He challenged us with questions and led with curiosity. He expected the same curiosity from us when it came to concepts around growing as people. He supported anyone who was struggling, and though he was an imposing physical presence, he possessed a sensitive, empathetic side that drew people in. He could bring humorous stories from his life experience when laughter was called for, yet he had the ability to turn deadly serious when he felt someone needed to hear something that they wanted to blow off. He knew that trying to do what we were trying to do at work was not commonly attempted, and he loved the idea of trailblazing and walking alongside us as we pushed the limits. He was forever a student of what made people tick, and he had a childlike fascination for what restaurant people actually did to earn a living!

12.

For Lou, creating something that resembled a therapy group would have felt about as good as getting a rectal exam; in his world, he alone was the proctologist. That's why he would never consider franchising. He had built his company based on his need to be the ultimate authority. He had the loudest voice and usually the only voice. He was not fond of feedback from his team. He saw the people around him the way Michael Jordan had described Scottie Pippen and the other Chicago Bulls—"his supporting cast." Lou was the sun, and the planets were allowed to revolve around him, as long as they didn't piss him off.

In contrast, I had found therapy essential. When I had physical issues, I'd see a doctor. I had emotional issues, so I saw a therapist. And Jeanne and I did marital counseling as well. I grew to believe that there are only two kinds of people in this world: those who are in therapy, and those who ought to be. Group provided all our key leaders the opportunity to learn conflict resolution skills, to embrace listening and communicating with one another in a new way. Since most of our team had grown up in similar homes to mine with at least a modicum of dysfunction, many felt the need to engage outside counselors to do their own deeper individual therapy. They, too, found that unpacking their childhood was critical in understanding why we act and speak in the ways we do. You may believe that people should keep their personal and professional lives separate. Though that may be the norm, I would say that it's not realistic, nor is it healthy.

Stories like mine offered clues from the past that inform my tendencies in the present. I panic over the thought of abandonment, which may have started when I, too, required surgery and a hospital stay as an infant in the days before mothers could stay in the hospital room overnight. It was likely exacerbated when my dad died young. I still become uneasy around anger and confrontation. I worry about living up to my dad's expectations. And I have a proclivity for introducing humor into any situation that begins to feel scary.

As a kid, my worst encounters with my dad were on the days when I had frustrated my mom to the point where she would clench her teeth and vow to tell Dad about it the second he got home. There was nothing scarier. I'd go to sleep knowing that he'd be home in a few hours, just as I was hitting my REM. The opening of the garage door would go off in my head like an explosion and suddenly I'd be awake. My dad would come into the house and walk upstairs where our bedrooms were, change from his suit into a robe, and go back down to the kitchen where Mom was cooking. Mostly, he reserved his anger for her, but occasionally she would avoid his wrath by telling him one of his sons, usually his firstborn, had done something bad. And right on cue, he'd yell, "MARC! Get down here!" My heart would be beating out of my ten-year-old chest with fear. I would literally forget how to tie words together to form sentences and could only manage a mumble as he interrogated me, asking such things as why I went to the mall after Mom had told me I couldn't. Or why I had hit a golf ball through the picture window of our neighbor, a police lieutenant? I wasn't a bad kid, but I was a kid. And Lou came home in the middle of the night after drinking Dewar's at Due all night, and it was anybody's guess what might happen.

I guess kids learn to tolerate their parents' behavior and usually believe that the things that occur in their home are normal—at least, until they are much older, and their eyes are opened to the reality of what actually happened. The home Rick and I grew up in was pretty sedate for twenty-three hours of every day, but that bewitching hour around three a.m. when Lou came home often became very loud and very scary. Lou would call Jean from the downtown restaurant as he was counting out the daily receipts and tell her to get the water boiling. He would be hungry, and he expected her to put a pasta dinner together for him from scratch in the time it would take him to drive home. She'd faithfully get out of bed and start cooking. He'd somehow drive himself home, avoiding police intervention, where he would be served a meal by his wife. Within minutes after finishing eating, he would start a loud argument, swearing at her and demeaning her.

Sometimes they'd only fight briefly, but on those nights when it went on too long and grew too scary, and Rick and I couldn't drown the sounds out by wrapping our pillows around our heads and humming, I would bravely fulfill my role as firstborn and go downstairs. Usually, I could distract my dad into a conversation about school or Little League and create a ceasefire. I was none too happy about getting up in the middle of the night, but anything was better than listening to him scream at my mom and hearing her cry. When he finally ran out of four-letter words, he'd leave the table and collapse in his bed upstairs. Little did I know that I would spend hundreds and hundreds of hours in therapy trying to work my way back through that battleground.

I was ten or twelve years old, with all kinds of questions about what all of that meant, and mostly I wondered if I was going to be OK. Was Mom going to leave? How could she not? Would she take me and Rick with her? Please don't leave us with Dad and let him start calling us those terrible names he called you! It seemed like they fought every night for years. After the noise had stopped, Rick and I grabbed a couple more hours of sleep before we needed to get ready for school. And then the thing that was truly crazy would happen—Mom wouldn't mention it.

Nada. Zero. She didn't know what to say. She made our lunches and kissed us goodbye.

I wish she would have said, "Everything's gonna be alright." Or "I'm sorry that we woke you." Again. Lie to us, but at least acknowledge that this is not normal. Married people argue, but this was Armageddon, and a little recognition of how it must have felt to an eight and twelve-year-old would have gone a long way. Even crazier was when we came home from school and watched as my mom was laying out my dad's clothing for him to wear to work, his fancy suit and his starched white shirt, tie, cufflinks, and shiny black leather shoes. We watched Mom and Dad chat as if they were allies. And then he left for work, only to return as the enemy about twelve hours later.

Here is what I've come to believe. If you're going to work with people every day, and spend lots of time together, you need to create a family at work that's not as crazy dysfunctional as the family you grew up in. In Group, we focused on working through here-and-now issues with one another in the circle. But sometimes, to get to the root of the fear and anger that we were projecting onto one another, we needed to go back to our family of origin. That work was best done with one's own individual therapist. In my therapy, I would need to relive these moments and feel the emotions all over again. But as an adult, I could give my feelings full expression and not hold everything in as I did as a child. I could speak all the anger and the fear and then let it go.

Over time, I learned that as convenient as it is to blame our parents and others for the things in our lives that keep us stuck, we must take our lessons and move on. Pointing my finger at others and being a victim doesn't ultimately lead me to change myself, the only person whom I can actually change. Nobody else can do it for me. If I continue to live with those issues in my life and don't get support to change, it's on me.

13.

Just a few months after we opened in River North, Stu and I discovered an old tavern called The Buffalo House that sat along a creek that ran through Buffalo Grove, in the northwest suburbs. We parked in the gravel lot against the front rail, which looked like a spot where Clint Eastwood would hitch his horse. A life-sized fiberglass buffalo stood chained to the porch, presumably so he wouldn't stampede. We walked through a rickety front door that should have been repaired sometime during Lincoln's presidency and into a place where, in the midst of the Ol' West ambience, we both had the entrepreneurial sensation of smelling money. Stu whispered, "We've gotta sell pizza here someday soon!"

We sat in the bar and could see into a small dining room off to the side. The place was a total dive, meaning you'd need to drop pretty low to consider it a mealtime option. The Buffalo House was the perfect choice if you had just played a doubleheader or painted your house on a hot day because you wouldn't feel bad about stopping in all sweaty and rank to have a cold one before you showered. If you were looking for somewhere to take a stale girlfriend on what would surely be your last date, this was your spot. I could almost imagine all the cowboys who had sat on my stool when real buffaloes still roamed the prairie here.

With each trip I made to The Buffalo House, our vision of a larger, cleaner, family-friendly roadhouse came more into focus. The place might have been beaten up and old, but both the building and the actual site carried a certain charm that made it unique. In my mind's eye, I could see thousands of new customers streaming into our fabulous new venue, one with GOLD MINE written all over it. There was only one minor issue—the homey little place was not for sale. We would need to dream up a unique strategy.

The Buffalo House stood on the corner of Lake Cook and Buffalo Grove roads. Next door was a three-and-a-half-acre plot of land, covered mostly by trees, and it was for sale. So, we hatched a plan: We had an architect sketch a rendering of a proposed giant Malnati's Pizzeria along with a two-hundred-spot parking lot on those vacant three and a half acres, which butted up against the older, smaller, soon-to-be-doing-less-business Buffalo House. Then Stu and I stopped in again for lunch. I asked our server to send the owner over when she had a chance. A few minutes later, a tall, dark-haired, serious woman approached our table. I introduced myself, handed her a business card, and unfurled the architect's drawing. I asked for her expert counsel on whether she thought the area would welcome a new family restaurant like Lou Malnati's.

Two days later, her husband called to say that he and his wife had been considering a sale of The Buffalo House. Would we want to meet for a cup of coffee before we got too far down the road with our plans for next door? Based on how aggressively he and his wife negotiated over the next several months, we clearly didn't scare them into a sale. They were doing well, but they also owned another restaurant, and they wanted to start slowing down. Looking back, if we had built that giant restaurant from the ground up on the neighboring lot, it likely would have bankrupted us. Instead, we struck a deal to buy their beautiful property. Once again, we asked them to be our bank and hold the mortgage for the $1 million acquisition.

The building was almost a century old—the second oldest in Buffalo Grove. Our architect did a masterful job of adding class to the structure without losing the yesteryear charm. He utilized corrugated metal painted to appear like copper with a worn-green patina. We oiled extra knotty cuts of oak flooring, which looked as if it had been there for a hundred years. We sourced a vintage scoreboard to replicate the one at Roemer Park in Wilmette, where we had played Little League baseball as kids. And we created a new home for our fiberglass buffalo under a sign that christened the place BuffaLou Malnati's. The restaurant looked fantastic, but we had gone way over budget. Fortunately, when we opened in the summer of 1988, we were welcomed by an onslaught of pizzaholics who had been waiting for us to find them out where the buffalo once roamed.

That proved a blessing, but deeply stressful, as once again the entire community decided to be the first on the block to give us a try. We did our best to accommodate everyone, but telling people it will be two hours for a carryout or three hours for a table is never the welcome guests want to hear. As I recall that opening, I shake my head and I'm without words; the memories of not being able to meet the demand percolate in my brain. It was like California in the summer—you couldn't put out the fires fast enough. When I'd tiptoe into the lobby, I'd wonder if any of these customers who had pushed their hunger off for hours before we told them that we had lost their order would ever return. In the kitchen, there were fully cooked pizzas stacked everywhere. Rick and Jimmy D'Angelo were working feverishly to pair up the pizzas with the tickets, but nothing matched! If there was an order for three pizzas, we could only find two. If the order was for a large with veggies, it somehow had sausage all over it.

Mix a thousand orders from five to seven with a brand new kitchen crew, and holy hell breaks out. But this, none of us had ever experienced anything like this. It was far worse than the Lincolnwood opening. And it was relentless. Day after day, night after night for months. And, oh . . . Jeanne and I had booked a trip to Italy eight months in advance, as

I was sure we would be open and under control by the time our vacation came around. But because of construction delays, we departed only three weeks after we opened. I was sure my brother would never talk to me again—with me gone, he couldn't come up for air.

Things weren't a lot better when we returned. And now it was reviewing time, when we would work through manager evaluations all day and then get to Buffalo Grove by 4:30 for the dinner rush. During the most intense stretch of business we had ever endured, one of our senior leaders threw his keys on my desk and quit after a second consecutive bad review. It got even more dicey, because in our family-centric little business, his sister was the GM of that struggling new Buffalo Grove store. She walked out when we wouldn't take her brother back after he changed his mind about quitting. Then a second brother, who was managing our Wilmette store, quit out of allegiance. Somehow, their father and stepmother stayed with the company, but this was one of Malnati's foundational families, and their leaving created seismic cracks in our infrastructure.

Losing three leaders at one time in a company with only a handful of stores pushed us to new limits. I was scared and frustrated, and I blamed myself. I wondered if this had occurred because I was trying to grow the business too fast. We had preached that we would expand only when our people were ready for new and bigger challenges, that people's preparedness would dictate the pace at which we opened new stores. But Buffalo Grove was our third new full-service restaurant in just over four years, and I worried that we had put too much pressure on our delicate balance, not allowing for the emotional fallout or physical burnout of some of our key players. I talked about it constantly to Jeanne, and those conversations helped me realize that as the leader, I had allowed relational issues to pile up and hadn't made enough time for the team to share their thoughts, feelings, and judgments with one another. In the midst of our busyness, we had skipped several of our monthly Group meetings. We had made the mistake of allowing the urgent to crowd out the most important.

Filling those leadership gaps was nearly impossible in the short-term, and it put pressure on all our stores because, to support the Buffalo Grove restaurant, we had to pull leaders from the others, and our bench was almost nonexistent.

Fortunately, Kathy Sullivan and Mike Schrager, the remaining managers at the restaurant, worked round the clock for months to get Buffalo Grove under control, while we patched up the team with a revolving door of managers from other stores. Finally, as the slower winter season arrived, we were able to take a collective breather. We got through the crisis. We reconnected our entire leadership team and swore we'd never risk coming unraveled like that again.

Losing people on whom you depend is never fun. In the restaurant business, the available temptations certainly add to the potential for bad behavior. There are always managers who run a little short of money and forget that your deposits are not actually theirs. We had a head cook who feigned shock when Rick discovered a full beef tenderloin on the front seat of her car. Catching people drinking from the beer tap in the banquet room was a fairly regular occurrence. Stealing and lying never look good, and the way I generally saw it, getting fired wasn't something that happened to you. You arranged it yourself.

There are times when someone demonstrates that while they work *for* you, they are not working *with* you. If you don't agree with how we are doing things or don't accept the decisions that are being made, we have a Group meeting, and we have the tools to deal with the conflict. Let's rip things up and hash them out, and after we've both been heard, we can hopefully move forward together in alignment. That's how leaders handle the situation. I have often been guilty of sticking with someone too long, working overtime to try to mend fences. Sometimes people change their attitudes and can learn to embrace what it means to be on a team. But there are other times when people are unwilling to shift, and though it's sad, it ends up being best to part ways.

The beauty of sitting in a circle together is that everyone feels as if he or she has a voice in the big decisions we have to make. Some called

Malnati's "a benevolent dictatorship," because while it was understood that the final decision rested with Rick and me, other people's ideas and opinions carried equal weight for us. With that philosophy, we have crushed industry norms around manager attrition, typically holding at 2–3 percent while most restaurant groups report losing 20 percent of their leaders yearly. Every year since 2010, the *Chicago Tribune* has picked top workplaces, the selections based largely on extensive surveying of employees. And every year since the inception, we have been selected.

We moved through those daunting times, leaning into the invincible work ethic of our people, and the new circle we had birthed together with Rich Blue. From a brand standpoint, Malnati's was coming into its own, and what hadn't killed us made us stronger. Financially, we had paid off all our debts, and our stores were all busy. And relationally, our team now understood that the work we were doing together in Group was paying dividends. We no longer imagined ourselves as part of a company. We had truly become a community.

14.

BEING A KID IN A restaurant family may keep you from going hungry, but the hours of operation guarantee that you will not receive the attention you might require. That was true for Rick and me, and it was also mostly true for my kids. While things had improved since the start of our marriage and I was no longer tied to Lincolnwood and out until all hours like my dad, as owner/operators, Rick and I were either working at one of our stores or on call and reachable in emergencies. The advent of car phones in the 1980s and then cell phones in the early 1990s didn't help. No escape. My family sometimes got the short end of the stick.

As a husband, I often had little left to offer Jeanne, so we sought out marriage counseling. My focus was usually on me and Malnati's as we grew from two outlets to seventy-two. My endless drive and need for success and special attention were issues that needed to be sorted out. I must have forgotten that I absolutely required her partnership for me to be successful. In counseling, I learned to stay better tuned into Jeanne, and I realized how valuable her feedback was to my growth.

In November 1987, our second daughter, Melissa, was born, and our family was complete. While I did the best I could to be present as a dad and as a husband, I typically felt like the juggler who is running around trying to keep those twelve plates all spinning on their poles at the same time. I knew I didn't want us to be a family where the kids suffer the consequences of a parent's career choice, but my presence was often spotty. I made sure we took family vacations. I tried to be home so we could eat dinner as a family or at least to tuck the kids in. But week in and week out, Jeanne carried the lion's share of the parenting, especially in those first ten to fifteen years of marriage, when we were building the foundation of Lou Malnati's. Fortunately, our kids had a mom who was always in their corner and was their biggest cheerleader, one who encouraged them by providing opportunities for them to become the best version of themselves.

Our youngest ended up getting a bigger chunk of me than both our older kids. Melissa was a happy child who laughed a lot, got along with everyone she met, and was wonderfully athletic. Though I had assisted some with Kelsey's and Will's teams, neither was notably interested in playing sports, and I like sports. Melissa was a natural who enjoyed having teammates and loved to compete. The Title IX law creating school athletic opportunities for women was passed in 1972, but the doors weren't really opened until the late 1980s and early 1990s.

That worked perfectly for Melissa and me, as I got to be her coach on an elite traveling softball team beginning when she was eight and continuing until she entered high school. She played both lacrosse and field hockey through four years of high school at New Trier. But when she entered college—like Kelsey, she followed Jeanne and me to Indiana—she needed a summer job, and we made our softball comeback together, coaching a team of younger girls for each of her four college summers. Our memories around those seasons on the diamond bonded us as a father and daughter. We took charge of a dozen girls and played in tournaments across the Midwest and taught them what it meant to be part of a team. The girls, in turn, taught me not to allow losing a game to define myself as a coach. These girls loved to win, but the thing they loved most was being with their friends. When we lost, they bounced back and were laughing together before we had put away the bats. I realized that losing no longer had to mean I was a loser, the belief I had carried since Flossmoor.

Melissa's friend and classmate, Elyssa Meyers, died by suicide in their sophomore year in high school. During Melissa's senior year, her former softball teammate, Ari Chester, was killed in a tragic automobile accident. Melissa worked in Malnati's HR department while she was getting her master's degree in social work, and I thought working in HR might attract her to a career at Malnati's. But helping others grieve the loss of friends became her calling. She became a director at the local nonprofit that Elyssa's parents founded to teach suicide prevention and led grief groups in local high schools and colleges. In 2015, she married Tom Molitor, her best friend from high school. Tom is a gifted videographer, and for years now his company, Dot Productions, has done incredible videos for Malnati's, as well as for his numerous other clients. Melissa and Tom have given us three grandchildren, Addison, Miles, and Eloise, who appear in cameos for the business as often as possible to raise the cuteness factor.

Our eldest, Kelsey, is compassionate and has a heart that has always gone out to others in need. When she was seven, she chose to give away most of her toys to kids in the inner city. For twelve months after college, she moved to Peru and worked at an orphanage for girls. She taught special education in the Chicago Public School system for a number of years, helping in an area that is perennially underfunded. She earned a master's in curriculum and instruction with a focus on English as a second language and created an improvement program for Malnati's Spanish-language staff members, giving many the support they needed to become managers. Where she sees a deficit, Kelsey seeks to fill it.

On a recent family trip to Mexico, Kelsey revealed that she was leaving her marriage of fourteen years, saying that she had bottled up her feelings and not shared her discontent with us because she had made herself believe that "Malnatis don't get divorced." Unfortunately, though she and her husband had worked long and hard with a therapist, she felt her marriage was beyond salvaging. Kelsey has three extraordinary kids—Lucy, Max, and Clara. Since they live only four blocks away, Jeanne and I are enjoying the privilege of being a part of their lives. Hopefully, they will soon work at Malnati's!

Kelsey now runs our family foundation, the Marc and Jeanne Malnati Family Foundation, which invests funds in nonprofits and neighborhood organizations, focusing on the disinvested South and West Sides of Chicago. She has helped us fashion a mission around supporting job training, violence reduction, education, and mental health, all meaningful themes for our family.

Our son, Will, was the most gregarious and outgoing of our kids. He seemed well-suited for a people-centric environment like Malnati's. He studied at the School of Hotel Administration at Cornell University and majored in hospitality. It seemed fair to assume that he would come back to Chicago after college to eventually take the baton from me in our family business, but it would be his call when that time would come.

After he graduated, he received an offer to begin his career in the Manhattan nightclub world, where he would be paid handsomely for a kid just out of school—far more than I would have paid him. He took the job, which allowed him to ride herd on some of the most cutting-edge venues in Gotham. He made lots of friends with actors, models, and the rich and famous. But when the nights that consistently ran past four a.m. burned him out after a few years, he returned to Chicago to help us open a new suburban restaurant in Lakewood. More on that later.

Jeanne and I had the opportunity to raise three fantastic kids. They are each bright and competent, and they are humble and care about other people. Each of them worked at Malnati's in different capacities as they grew up. But we always left it up to them to choose their ultimate career. I don't think working with your father is a simple proposition. If Lou hadn't died, would I have been excited to work with him? To work *for* him? It might not have been pretty. I surely wouldn't have wanted to do it *his* way. With our kids, I thought that if I didn't push too hard, one of them might choose to follow me.

At age thirty-seven, once our kids were in school full-time, Jeanne enrolled part-time in the School of Social Work at Loyola University Chicago. She scored straight A's every semester except the one in which she had two gall bladder surgeries—quite the achievement. Upon graduation, she built her private practice, seeing individuals and leading therapy groups and retreats. We hired her at Malnati's, where she facilitated the monthly Group for directors in our home office for ten years.

One of the best lessons that Jeanne has taught our family is that relationships don't disintegrate when someone purposely says something you don't want to hear. In a family, as well as in business, the failure to share something that's eating at you in a relationship begins to create a barrier. But it's subtle. The barrier is built one brick at a time. The time you were late and left me hanging, but I let it go. The time you told someone something I had shared with you in confidence, but I shrugged it off as no big deal. Brick by brick a disconnect is built. A wall grows so high you can't see one another over the top. And just like that, your relationship is in the ICU, and the job of breaking up all that settled mortar is both difficult and frightening.

She emphasized the importance of acknowledging your fear of offending someone and going a step further to have the difficult conversation. The principle is counterintuitive, the opposite of what I'd naturally believe. But experience has taught me that saying what you think someone may not want to hear typically builds trust instead of rancor.

Jeanne loved the work we were doing at Malnati's, and as our kids became more independent, she set out to bring the story and the principles to other businesses, nonprofits, and churches. She started her own business called The Culture Group. As a passionate and gifted speaker, she spoke to groups all around the country. She would challenge her audience to share their feelings and to risk having honest conversations. And she supplied them with communication tools to help transform their workplace culture.

15.

You may have started to think that I put the restaurant business on hold while I enrolled in eight or ten years of therapy. While that
would have been beneficial for my insecure, underdeveloped sense of
self, I did continue working, and we built some very cool restaurants in
these next several years. There were times, though, that work was not
just about pleasing our guests and producing great pizza. There were all
kinds of personal, existential questions that seemed to be popping up in
places and at times when I didn't expect them. Therapy can do that. It
opens a box that resists being shut again. That happened on the day we
opened our largest restaurant to date in downtown Naperville.

It was Valentine's Day 1994, and we had leased the former city center fire station, which had the look of a bland office building. Since we
always tried to give each restaurant a unique appearance and personality,
bland wasn't acceptable. We strive to create interest with the feel of a
restaurant and pair that with friendly, neighborhood service and food
that is addictive. We believe that will provide us with a better mousetrap
and help attract thousands of people every week. To that end, we constantly tasked our creatively gifted architect, Mark Knauer, and his team
to dream big with us.

Mark imagined a hundred-year-old vintage, slide-down-the-pole fire station. It would have oversized bright red garage doors. There would be a fireplug in the lobby, a full-sized model mannequin of a little boy crouching on a rescue trampoline, and firehouse memorabilia everywhere. If the building didn't resemble a vintage firehouse, we would reimagine it as one. Because my lifelong friend Tim Anderson was in the process of launching his own company, Focus Development, I asked him to help with what would be a giant undertaking. Tim ran point on negotiating a fair deal with the property's owner, Norm Rubin, a major land baron in Naperville. He then managed the construction on this project and built the next dozen restaurants for us.

On opening night, I recall that I was walking proudly from the kitchen toward the front door as the sound system cranked "Bang the Drum All Day," by Todd Rundgren. I was just about to flip open the lock on the firehouse doors to let the local populace get their first taste of their new Malnati's. And right as I approached the host station, an accusing little voice in my head posed the question: "Is all this about living out your dream, Marc, or is it really your dad's dream that you're living?" I tried to swat the query away, as if a hornet had landed on my ear. Instantly I felt my joy receding. An internal argument ensued.

"Don't listen to that shit. Your biggest, most beautiful restaurant to date is about to open after fifteen months of hard-fought negotiation, design, redesign, and winter construction. You should be thrilled! Exhilarated! The waiting is over!"

But there it came again. "Hey! Wasn't it Lou who wanted to build restaurants across America? Wasn't it Lou who professed to be the Ray Kroc of pizza?"

In opening more stores, was I demonstrating that I had allowed my father to program me to live out the destiny that he wasn't able to? Was I just a puppet? A clone of Lou? I started to perspire heavily.

Then I reminded myself that being in this business, building out a world-class team, and surrounding myself with people who truly cared about one another was something that I loved. And having a chance to make people happy day in and day out by preparing the best pizza anywhere . . . these were *my* dreams. And I was doing it much differently than my dad would have done it.

By the time I reached the front door, the smile had sniggled its way back onto my face. I was hugely relieved to have that purpose-confirming conversation with myself in the four seconds it took to walk from the kitchen to the front door. At the same time, I noticed that I was bending my dad's voice into one that was mocking me, and I wanted to put that voice to bed for good, if that was possible.

I did much of that work with a therapist named Bob Slone. Slone would allow me to make him into a representation of Lou, who had been dead for twenty years, and give me the chance to talk to him. To say the things I couldn't say as a boy, for fear of getting whacked in the mouth. Slone would put a big leather chair between us and give me a wiffle bat to help access my feelings, anger first. Anger serves as a sort of gateway emotion that will lead to deeper feelings of fear and sadness. Then Slone would playact Lou, and I would talk to him, scream at him. When I'd run out of words, Slone would coach me to use sounds or grunt and swing the bat down on the chair from high above my head—as long as I didn't hit him. Slone explained that the old feelings were still present in my body, and that this was a method to gain access.

I threw all the same words back at Lou that he had used to terrorize my mom. The amount of venom and wrath stored up inside was astonishing. I realized that I could be as angry and scary as my father, and I felt the power in demonstrating it physically and verbally. There seemed to be layer after layer to the anger that I had stored up. For days after a session, my hands would be blistered from pounding relentlessly on the chair, and my throat would be sore and raspy. I'd get to a point where I couldn't imagine I had anymore left to say or feel, and then with the surfacing of a different memory, a new torrent would present itself.

I learned that anger would exist in me whether I wanted it or not.

What mattered was that I was aware of it and could choose how to mete it out; I had to stop pretending things were fine when I was upset. Trying to be a people-pleaser. The answer to not becoming like Lou had never been to stuff my anger, as I learned to do as a boy, but rather to acknowledge its presence and learn to express it responsibly. I learned that anger lived on a continuum that ranged from mild frustration to full-blown rage. I was carrying rage from having been bullied and from seeing my mom and brother bullied. The reason I had been so scared of being even mildly angry must have been my fear of tapping down into that reservoir deep below the surface and not being able to stop the rage from erupting like lava from a volcano.

Slone taught me that anger is not bad; rather it's like a warrior with a powerful sword. He knows when to show the sword while keeping it sheathed, and he knows when to bring it out as a last resort. I learned that holding back on one's anger causes major internal plumbing problems. When "the pipe" from which feelings flow is pinched off, all our feelings are impacted. Life loses its color and becomes dull. We can't be known or know ourselves without the ability and the willingness to fully feel.

Therapy helped me begin to move toward fuller expression and helped me eventually realize that my dad had done the best he could with the hand he had been dealt. His dad was absent for most of his formative years. He learned discipline in the Marine Corps. Slone helped me see that my father had loved me. That's the message I had been chasing my whole life and my entire career in his namesake business. I came to believe that he would have been proud of the job I had done to grow the business. That he would be OK with me doing it differently than he would have. What I had to accept was that Lou was no longer around to give me any of those blessings that I desperately desired. Instead, I would have to learn to give them to myself. That also made it easier to appreciate and respect him for handing off a great business and a uniquely spectacular product.

16.

THE FIRST TIME I VISITED the location in North Lawndale that would become our tenth restaurant, we had to wade through the garbage that was strewn all over the floor. The site was a former grocery store that had been closed for at least five years. It smelled terrible, and the flies were attacking in droves. Like so many other buildings in the once proud area, it had a brick structure, so the bones were good, but it had suffered from serious neglect. The basement had taken on water because the pump wasn't operable, and there were traces of rat habitation. The store did not have its own parking lot, and parking in the area seemed to be at a premium.

The demographics indicated that Lawndale was a well-populated, mostly African American neighborhood on Chicago's Near West Side, but the average income was low and the crime rate was among the highest, not only in Chicago, but in the country. Everything our real estate consultant had taught us after the Flossmoor debacle began with "location, location, location." I didn't dare show her this one—I could already hear her screaming, "NOOO! Don't do it!! Get back in your car and drive away!" So what exactly precipitated this visit in 1995 to a neighborhood that had never been close to being a spot on our location wish list?

It started with Rick deciding to become a part-time assistant for Mel Sheets, his high school basketball coach at New Trier. Rick knew that for New Trier to become more competitive and ready to play for that elusive state championship, the team had to schedule games against some tough city schools. He also thought that giving his suburban white kids exposure to black kids from the city could be potentially beneficial to both groups. He knew Wolf Nelson, the basketball coach at Farragut High School in Lawndale, and together they decided to play a game every year and then have the teams get together socially afterward for pizza. It worked out well. The formula created a win-win learning experience for all involved.

During one of the games, Wayne "Coach" Gordon, the ex-wrestling coach at Farragut turned pastor, met Rick and struck up a friendship. Rick found him to be one of the most courageous men he had ever met. Coach Gordon had left Farragut a few years prior to start a storefront church, with many of his athletes becoming the first congregants. A one-time football player and a divinity student at Wheaton College, he and his wife, Anne, moved into North Lawndale to make a difference, to stand in the gap against racial inequality (the Gordons are white) and be a voice for marginalized folks who don't often have a voice of their own. Together, Coach Gordon and Anne raised their family there and grew a powerful church that went on to birth a giant health center, a community development office, legal and counseling practices, a neighborhood health club, and Hope House, a home for men desiring to turn their lives around after incarceration or being broken by drug use.

One day, Coach asked Rick if he and I would meet with him about a big opportunity. We drove down to this area of Chicago that I had read about but never visited. Sitting in his office, Coach told us that he had polled people in his congregation, the Lawndale Community Church, and the results showed that high atop the list of things they felt their neighborhood needed was a sit-down restaurant where people could celebrate birthdays and anniversaries, have business lunches, or just get a good meal. Lawndale had been devastated by the rioting and looting after the assassination of Martin Luther King Jr. in 1968. Businesses and buildings had been burned to the ground, and nearly thirty years later they had not been rebuilt. A restaurant such as what Coach was proposing did not exist in the neighborhood.

Coach looked us in the eyes and said, "I've been thinking and praying about our meeting today. I read up on you on your website and noticed that you currently have nine locations. Do you happen to understand the principle of 'tithing' that God introduced to protect the poor in the Old Testament?"

Our parents were generous, and they had raised us to be generous, so we understood that we had a responsibility to care for others who were less fortunate, but we didn't know where he was going with this. Coach continued: "The principle lives on today. And it's not only people who are called by God to tithe, but businesses are as well. Since the next store you open will be your tenth, would you consider tithing it back to our community, a place that is in great need? You can say yes to North Lawndale and bless this neighborhood. You can even have your new location free of rent!" The church owned the building.

Coach had thrown down the God Card. How could we possibly say no to Coach and to God?

From a business standpoint, it was impossible to justify making a move like this. Maybe we could just write a nice check, and that would suffice or at least allow us to walk away from this meeting without too much guilt. Rick and I didn't commit and told Coach we would sleep on it. On our way home, I spat out at least a hundred reasons why we couldn't do this project. Rick just listened, because he was torn. He had just married Tina Chiropoulos, a fun-loving young woman whom he had met way back when she worked with us at ChicagoFest when she was only fifteen. Being a new husband as well as a part-time basketball coach, he knew he would have little time to invest in the establishment of this potential new restaurant.

Later that week, Jeanne and I packed up our kids and joined our friend Dave Gotaas Jr. and his family for the trip of a lifetime to Africa. The timing was perfect, as it created space for me to seek some divine insight on tithing our tenth location to Lawndale.

We traveled to the Maasai Mara National Reserve in Kenya and went on a safari that exceeded all our expectations. The land was incredible, and the people were warm and welcoming, though most had very little in the way of possessions. But it was in Nairobi, when we walked through the Kibera slum, where over a million people live virtually on top of one another in abject poverty, that God really got my attention. I felt His gentle nudge to lend our support where support was most needed at home. I was clearly reminded how He had blessed us after we climbed out of the Flossmoor hole with fabulous opportunities in Schaumburg and Buffalo Grove, where we were able to buy valuable real estate, having neither credit nor collateral. God had been more than faithful to us, and we had seen our business grow. Now, as always, His timing on the Africa trip had been impeccable. We would give the Lawndale project the thumbs up.

I appealed to our vendors for support, and they came through in a big way. E.J. Industries donated all the booths for the dining room, and Boelter helped us with our kitchen equipment package. The Coca-Cola Company paid for a reproduction of artwork on a giant metal billboard featuring the Harlem Globetrotters drinking Cokes; the mid-1950s original was thought to be the first instance of Black athletes appearing in a sports marketing ad. Friends donated cash to the church to help get the building back in shape. Drew Goldsmyth, a contractor and life-long Lawndale resident, led the reconstruction project, and by working eighteen-hour days, made it come together on a shoestring.

The day before we planned to open, in the summer of 1995, Drew and I were on our knees in the doorway tacking down carpet strip, when a car screeched around the corner and drove full throttle through a stockade fence in the empty lot across the street. Several loud gunshots followed, and as I incredulously looked over at Drew, a former Marine, I saw him rolling away for cover. I slammed the door shut and sat there waiting for the replay so I could make sense of what we'd just witnessed. A little while later, when the dust had cleared, I asked Drew if he thought we should walk across the street and see if anyone was hurt. He looked back at me with his head shaking side to side, and half-laughingly said, "You're in the 'hood, son. We don't go lookin' for trouble 'round here."

Lawndale didn't turn a profit for ten years. As a matter of fact, we invested over $1 million to stay afloat and keep the doors open as the new beacon of light in the community. We were given awards as Chicagoans of the Year by *Chicago* magazine editor-in-chief Richard Babcock in 1998, and the *Chicago Tribune* ran a front-page feature on the restaurant as well. We were able to provide an avenue to the job market through job training for some of the men who lived in the church-run Hope House, teaching them skills such as cooking or operating our point-of-sale computer system. We may not have been winning financially, but Pastor Gordon asked us not to give up on "their" Lou Malnati's because it was having a huge emotional effect on his adopted community. God had continued to bless all our other stores, so we stayed the course.

The Lawndale store was only three blocks from the home of Myrtle Pearson, who had been one of the first veteran pizza chefs to leave Pizzeria Due and come to work in Lincolnwood with my dad. Myrtle was an incredible cook, who never cracked under pressure and had a huge heart for developing people. She personally taught every management trainee the fine points of preparing and cooking a perfect pizza, and she won them over with her hearty laugh. Myrtle was delighted that her workplace was now a part of her very own neighborhood, and she jumped at the opportunity to work the last few years of her storied career at the helm of the Lawndale kitchen.

A modicum of profitability was ultimately due to our ability to begin home delivery. When we first opened, nobody would even apply for a delivery driver job. It was far too dangerous, and people feared they would get robbed. But eventually crime subsided and relative safety was established. It was a warm feeling then, and still is now, to imagine that we have been contributors to the progress of the neighborhood. Over the years, the profits came and went, but when we earned some—as promised—we donated them back to educational and recreational programs for kids through the church. Opening in Lawndale had been a good idea for reasons that weren't so obvious on the surface, but we knew we had been called to set an example for other businesses to follow.

17.

RICK WAS ALWAYS A GUY who came up with multiple ideas daily.
Some were crazy, many required too much investment for the potential
payback, but some were absolute genius. While Lawndale was great for
our spirit, Tastes of Chicago, our e-commerce company, paid big dividends financially and put us on the map nationally.

Like many good ideas, it was the daughter of necessity. It started
with Rick's frustration over the fact that we had festivals that created
additional revenue in the summer months, but we didn't have anything
like that in the winter. For years, he had watched our customers pack
their coolers with pizzas when they were traveling. When he asked
about it, they said they were following the demands of their out-of-state
friends and relatives: "Don't even bother coming without bringing Malnati's!" So we would give their pizzas a partial bake, wrap them in foil,
and set them off on their journeys.

Sometime in the late 1980s, Rick noticed that Federal Express was
providing overnight shipping service. He approached the company and
asked if it was shipping any food items and found that Legal Seafood
in Boston and a bakery in New Orleans had recently become their first
restaurant clients. FedEx saw the potential for pizza and was helpful in

getting us to a place where we could ship. With winter coming, Rick instructed our servers to alert our dining room customers that, for one day only, we would be shipping pizzas for delivery anywhere in the country to arrive before Christmas Eve. We attached flyers to all our carryout and delivery orders as well. We got a fantastic response, shipping nearly four hundred individual orders that year.

Rick had tested dry ice in the restaurant, and it seemed to keep the pizzas frozen for almost forty-eight hours. What we hadn't done was subject it to the bumping up and down in a FedEx truck or to traveling in the heat of the Southern states. We didn't use Styrofoam for that first shipment, and without it, the dry ice melted faster than we anticipated, and the corrugated box didn't hold up structurally. There must have been at least fifty complaints when the pizzas arrived warm or in broken packaging. And because Rick was managing the project tightly, he had forwarded the customer service phone number to his home phone. Rick didn't make it to our family's Christmas dinner that year as he personally fielded call after call.

Despite that early glitch, the business grew to the point where we shipped packages every Wednesday, and we were slowly able to hire a staff. We made the pizzas in our bigger stores, freezing them, and finally gathering them to ship out of a central hub in Northbrook. There was no team yet to pack the pizzas into boxes and load them on the FedEx truck, so the people who worked in the office did it. On big days, we'd recruit our managers and our best people from the stores to come in before or after their shift to help as well. Like everything else we did, the leaders took the project on together, and because of our collective desire to see our pizza win, the long hours and assembly line work was a price we were willing to pay. Maybe we believed that if our pizza became more significant, we would gain the human significance we were all chasing, because we always seemed to add work and seldom found ways to reduce it.

We started to advertise over the holidays on local radio stations like WGN and The Loop. Our family had fun going into the studio to create commercials touting great pizza, a family company, and

1-800-LOU-TO-GO—a simple call that would allow people to ship pizza overnight to feed relatives, make friends, to settle losing bets. When Peter Jennings and *World News Tonight* picked up on the story of iconic restaurants starting to ship food nationally, it gave us the boost we needed to believe that this little business, our side hustle, could blossom into something much bigger.

As companies were first beginning to dabble with the idea of utilizing the internet as a marketplace to sell their product, we decided to go all-in and dedicated the resources to investigate how that might happen. It seems so simple now, but this was the dawning of the age, and Amazon had only been operating out of Jeff Bezos's garage for a year and a half and was only selling books. In 1997, we lined up our domain name, found a company that would clear our sales, and built our first website. This type of e-commerce was new, and it would take a minute for people to begin to trust this way of buying, but it looked promising.

In the early 2000s, we changed the name from Lou Malnati's Priority Pizza to Tastes of Chicago, echoing the name of the popular food festival that had meant so much to our company. We rented an approved U.S. Department of Agriculture kitchen from our friend Joe Perrino, of Home Run Inn, the popular South Side pizza chain. We brought on Vienna Beef and Carson's Ribs as additional offerings. Eli's Cheesecake and Garrett's Popcorn followed, as we set out to provide more than just Chicago pizzas and to ship all the foods that made Chicago such a mouthwatering foodie town. Eventually, Portillo's, Lettuce Entertain You, and Gibsons Steakhouse all came on board, as did a host of other local favorites. The business grew through the painstaking efforts of Sally Glunz, Mindy Kaplan, and Stu Cohen. We celebrated our first single day of shipping one thousand packages, then five thousand, then ten thousand. Then there was that first December day when we worked from 4 a.m. to 6 p.m. and shipped $1 million worth of food! What had seemed inconceivable had become reality and given our little Chicago family company the ability to reach other families from coast to coast.

18.

In late 1996, when my brother told me he was leaving the company, I was deeply sad. As complementary partners for fifteen years, we had often approached business issues from different perspectives. Rick was more conservative, satisfied with the number of stores we were operating, and I was always ready to grow and expand, dreaming about the great restaurants we still needed to open. He always had a pile of uncashed paychecks in his desk, while I had spent every penny of mine and then borrowed some more as Jeanne and I were raising three kids. But though we might have had different perspectives, we would typically end up in the same place on most decisions.

Looking back, though, I think it may have been the decision to buy Buffalo Grove right after opening Schaumburg and River North that was ultimately too much for him. The ferocity with which people stormed the doors when we opened put him over the edge. After that, he had had enough. He liked the restaurant business, but too often it felt like a job to him. He was great at it, but it didn't lie within what author and psychologist Gay Hendricks refers to as a "zone of genius"—that sweet spot where you're doing work that both utilizes your natural gifts and brings you joy and fulfillment. Rick only found that when he was mentoring kids and helping them learn to play basketball.

He asked himself, "When the days get long, and the stress ramps up, do I still love the challenge of managing through it in the restaurant business? Or am I dreaming of a different future that doesn't involve trying to satisfy the hunger of hundreds of people all at once every day?" That was the dilemma for Rick. He knew from his younger days when he had run a summer sports camp with Scott Weiner that he loved working with kids and having an influence on their lives. And basketball had always been his passion. So when the opportunity came to return to our old high school as the boys' head basketball coach, he knew it was the perfect calling for him. He became a world-class coach, making New Trier High School a perennial state powerhouse, and he got the added benefit of teaching physical education in the place where his talented kids, Tino, Gaby, and Gianna, would go to school. They each played high school basketball and wore the same "21" as their dad had worn in his playing days. Tino even went on to play in the Big Ten at Northwestern.

It wouldn't be the same at Malnati's without Rick. On the one hand, his reluctance to expand would likely have created conflicts between us. It's not good to drive with one foot on the gas and the other on the brake. But he was a good governor for me. He made me evaluate and then reevaluate, and I needed that sort of discipline, because I could be impulsive and too willing to see the upside only, or to give the upside far more weight than the potential downside. I could be persuasive, but he would stand up to me when few others would. I asked him if he made this decision because I was too controlling, and he assured me that he was just following his passion. But in the wonderings and wanderings of my own mind, I realized that he would become the second important male in my life to leave me, and I couldn't help feeling the pangs of abandonment once again. What was God trying to teach me? I didn't have an answer.

I hoped that maybe Rick would try coaching for a short while, and then decide to come back, so I left the door open, and he remained my business partner. He and I have a curious but unbreakable bond. As kids, we had endured the terror of our family's dysfunction together. We had walked on the same eggshells and pretended that everything was normal. We were one another's security blankets. Survival creates a glue that can't be easily broken. Rick and I had always been together, and I was scared about whether I'd still like running the business without him by my side.

I decided that the only chance I'd have to ease my loneliness would be to increase the small circle of leaders I could confide in and run ideas past. This would also have the effect of constructing a stronger and wider leadership structure that could support Malnati's expansion into the future. That team became Stu, our former accountant; Jim Freeland, the chef from CIA; and district managers Jimmy D'Angelo, who had started as a busboy; his younger brother, Dennis D'Angelo, a pro baseball wannabe; and Kathy Sullivan, a registered nurse who didn't like hospitals. I believed this team would become the champions of our culture—leaders who could communicate our vision clearly, develop our restaurant managers, and coach their stores to greater profitability. Unlikely characters can sometimes create just the right chemistry to build a special company.

Jim D'Angelo started his career at Malnati's at fifteen, when his older brother Joe, who was part-time in Elk Grove's kitchen, told him to come into work because we were short. Jim didn't love school, but he found that he loved to work for a couple of reasons in particular. First, Jim is a learner, and with his dark complexion, jet black hair, and a proclivity for picking up Spanish, he fit in easily with our veteran Hispanic cooks. He made them teach him everything. And second, though he professed to be shy around girls, he met one named Laura Syperski, who worked the phones at Elk Grove, and the more he worked, the more he got to see Laura.

By nineteen, he was the youngest employee ever awarded a key to the store by Peachy, who trusted him to open or close in a pinch. Jim and Laura worked hard and saved money. She had become a stellar server, and he had moved into management when they got married and bought a townhome in Schaumburg near where they worked. As Jim would tell the story, "It was about twenty minutes after we bought our house when Marc called me to ask if I'd run the struggling River North store for a year to see if I could turn it around. I was a suburban kid who had only ventured downtown two or three times in my life. I said, 'No way.'"

But we knew that we needed to turn River North around fast or we would have to close it. And we believed that Jim was a guy who could make a difference because of his work ethic and his ability to influence people. Rick was still with us, and he called Jim, who was going to college part-time. "Jimmy, if you want to grow, you've got to live in your uncomfortable zone," Rick told him. "School is important, but it can wait. You've only earned two years of credits in three years anyway. When you're ready to go back, we'll help you. This is the time to choose career." I'm pretty sure Rick quoted the great thought leader Yogi Berra and told Jim, "Whenever you see the fork in the road, take it!"

Jim didn't like it, but he knew Rick was right. He dropped out of college and took the position. Though he had not been a general manager before, he was able to get things going in a much better direction, and he took advantage of the fact that the neighborhood began to enjoy a grand resurgence. The promise of one year soon turned into three, but in that time, Jim established himself firmly as a leader who didn't shy away from big challenges.

He followed this stint by playing a critical role in establishing Buffalo Grove and was subsequently chosen to be the opening GM of Naperville before assuming his district manager role. (In our system, a general manager handles one store, a district manager oversees seven or eight stores, and a regional manager oversees a handful of district managers.) His early decision paid off, as he eventually reentered school at thirty-five years old, taking classes part-time around his restaurant duties, and graduated from the University of Illinois Chicago at forty! All five of Jim and Laura's kids have worked at Malnati's. Laura's sister, Kerri, has been our GM in Schaumburg for 20 years. All in, there were more than twenty Malnati employees that emanated from their extended family. Jim would Jim would become the COO of Lou Malnati's in 2012 and lead our entire store-level operations team.

In 1998, as Rick was leaving, Jim became my right-hand man when it came to running the restaurants. He was respected across the company for being a straight shooter who had a way of telling people things they didn't want to hear and getting them to love him for it. He was compassionate but honest, and because he didn't try to hide any of his own faults, he made it easier for people to embrace their own. Over the years, he and I created opportunities to lead assorted teams in tandem, allowing our beliefs about business and life to blend so that our message and vision almost always sounded the same.

Jimmy D.'s brother Dennis became our first DM for the standalone carryout stores. That business had started slowly, but had become a profit center as the convenience of having a nearby option for delivery and carryout increased over the years. Dennis's dream of pitching in the major leagues ended when he blew out his elbow in college—throwing way too many breaking balls as a seven-year-old has a way of doing damage over time. Once he graduated, we quickly recruited him onto our Malnati softball team and told him that he could also manage our Northbrook carryout shop. The store hadn't run well since our manager was spotted selling marijuana to minors in the park across the street, so Dennis's timing was perfect.

He turned out to be a stellar addition. He was a stickler for doing things the right way, and the same way every time, just as he had learned to perfect his pitching mechanics. He became the guy who opened each of our new carryout stores. (By the time the company turned fifty, there were nearly fifty of them.) Dennis made sure that the training continued until everyone on the team knew their role, and until the pizza was consistently excellent. These small operations, which had grown to between 1,600 and 1,800 square feet in size, had become big producers, and they often brought in over $1,000 a square foot in revenue annually, which is far above the retail standard. Dennis made them run with the precision of a Simone Biles routine.

With his leadership, we started opening more carryout/delivery stores in areas around our restaurants, using a hub-and-spoke approach. Our goal for growth was to open restaurants in the denser areas of Chicagoland and install these carryouts with full kitchens but no seats in the smaller suburban villages.

Dennis was famous throughout the company for being the guy who would work all day, visit stores through dinner, kiss his family goodnight, return his emails, and then, as his clock struck midnight, he'd start his two-hour daily weight training. He is a unicorn in the pizza business, as he has never allowed himself to have anything but a six-pack for thirty years, and I don't mean beer. He even had a run-in with cancer, and the cancer just said, "Fahgetaboutit. He's too tough for me."

Dennis became our systems guy, and along with the carryouts, he standardized our operations at festivals, in the Tastes of Chicago shipping department, and in kitchens across the company. He redeveloped the cooking process for our thin-crust pizzas and took them to a whole new level of delicious. He currently serves as a regional manager, responsible for more than thirty stores and reporting to his brother.

Kathy Sullivan worked her way through nursing school by bartending in the city and by working as a server at Pizzeria Due. She joined us in the mid-1980s as she was just finishing nursing school, but she never quite got around to becoming a nurse. The restaurant business was in her blood, and she thrived in it. She was smart, didn't panic in a crisis, and she was a skilled multitasker. She was a ballbuster when the situation required it and never subscribed to the theory about women being the weaker sex. Most guys in the company were scared to death of incurring the wrath of The Warden.

Kathy, or Sully, as we called her, helped us open Schaumburg and then stepped into the GM role that was vacated during the crisis in Buffalo Grove. She was an excellent trainer who had a keen eye for talent, a skill critical to growing a company. Her internal jury would convene after observing someone's work habits and quickly determine whether they would be great or too soft. She was always ready with feedback and would share it unabashedly. She didn't pull punches, even with me. She had the sense of humor of a truck driver, and she could mix it up with a group of men without ever blushing.

One time making a store visit, she heard loud mariachi music coming from the kitchen. Instead of asking the cooks to turn it down again because guests could hear it in the dining room, she thought she'd make a point. She asked who owned the old banged-up, duct-taped boom box. When one of the guys responded that it was his, she asked what he thought it was worth in its compromised condition. He said probably about five bucks. Kathy pulled out a $10 bill and asked if he'd sell it to her. "*Si!*" he said with a big smile. Kathy pulled the plug and flung the contraption into the dumpster.

After she became a district manager, Kathy rode herd on our point-of-sale vendor and solved most of our computer problems. It was her idea to split our pizza lines on busy nights, so that one crew handled the dining room and another worked carryout and delivery, which made for a vast improvement in the number of pizzas we could handle efficiently at one time. She was a solid problem solver who quickly grew impatient when things weren't running well. And though she showed a bulletproof exterior, she had a sweet and sensitive side that drew people in. When Sully retired, she received a painting of a magnificent tree with many branches, with a name assigned to each branch denoting the thirty-plus managers Sully had hired or developed during her career, some from her own family.

Having multiple family members on our team put us at risk, as we experienced when three sibling leaders left at once during the opening of Buffalo Grove. Other times we had to deal with people who felt that a family member was being treated with favoritism. There are plenty of reasons not to risk nepotism.

But the positives of families coming together to create one big Malnati Family outweighed the negatives. Families hold one another accountable. They push each other to grow. And, of course, they cover shifts for one another. They are foundational to our culture, and when the next generation comes along, parents have a safe place for their kids to work and learn the principles of being part of a community. But when family intersected with Group, and we were charged with holding each of our Group members accountable, it added a little wrinkle to the process. One such occurrence reared its ugly head when Sully found her nephew drinking at work.

19.

As a young manager, Mike Schrager was living with one foot in his restaurant career and another back in college. Mike was smart and talented and had good people skills, but he had grown up on Chicago's Near North Side in a hard-partying Irish Catholic community, where most of his friends and his friend's friends drank too much. His nickname was Bagel and he resembled one—a solid fifty pounds overweight. He had worked his way up into a GM role after fifteen years, but he was struggling to handle the responsibility. Mike was Kathy's nephew, and at this point, he reported to her.

Kathy caught Mike drinking during his day shift in Elk Grove. He didn't get defensive, because she caught him red-handed. He admitted that his drinking was a problem, but he believed he could stop. She told him he could do that, but she wasn't willing to hold his secret. She told him that he would need to own up to it with our leadership team during our scheduled Group meeting the next morning.

Mike told the circle how bad things had turned, swore he'd quit, and begged to keep his job. Rick and I had lived with an alcoholic, but we didn't have much experience supporting one's recovery. The rest of the group had varied levels of exposure and lots of feelings were expressed.

The group suggested that if he had even a chance to continue at Malnati's, Mike would have to attend ninety AA meetings in ninety days and never drink again. Seventy percent of addicts relapse at some point and most within the first year, so by taking on this challenge, it would show us that he understood that he had strayed off the path and was serious about finding his way again. He agreed to sign up for a three-year program of weekly group counseling with Rich Blue along with the addiction meetings. He was suspended from work, and we made no promises that we'd take him back. We only told him that if he didn't see his challenges through, he would have zero future with Malnati's.

I'm generally easy-going, but I'm not exempt from an occasional Malnati family incendiary moment. In this case, I remember my reaction distinctly. My breathing was short and quick, and I was feeling rage. Mike had put our company at risk, working and leading our people while intoxicated. How long had it been going on? My jaw was like stone and my eyes attempted to bore a laser hole through his face. When it was my turn to share, I told him what I thought of him, and I gave it to him double-barrel. If it caused him more shame, perfect. I showed little compassion, and I told him I didn't think he'd complete the ninety meetings in ninety days. I added that I wasn't sure I wanted to see him again anyway.

What was spoken in Group, stayed in Group. But we were free to discuss our own reactions to issues if we didn't disclose names or stories. I went home that night and told Jeanne that I had lost it when the subject of drinking at work came up. She sat and listened to me, and wondered out loud if I was reacting to my past. I then realized that only a small percentage of my anger had been about Mike and that most of it had focused on my memories of my dad's drinking. Sure, Mike had embarrassed Malnati's and likely created some risk for the company. But it wasn't even close to the risk my dad had created for our family through his obsession with alcohol. I saw clearly then that my old resentment of Lou had resurfaced. Those feelings were just lying there, dormant, in the abyss of my soul, waiting for someone like Mike to dial up that same frequency on my internal radio so I could pounce, projecting my anger for Lou onto him. So crazy.

Fortunately, the team was much more even-handed with Mike. The Group worked to create consequences that "fit the crime," wanting to love and support Mike as a member of the circle, but also to push him hard to make the big changes that were necessary in his life. If he could do that, we'd have a far different person on the other side, one who was sober, had more self-respect, and through painful self-examination would re-earn his place in our community.

Shame is driven by secrets. "We're only as sick as our secrets" is a standard recovery principle. Sully was brilliant in making Mike come clean with everyone right away. It's not the things we say, but the things that we withhold that can do the most internal damage. Like a bad sliver, the whole thing has to come out before healing can begin. That's where having the Group to unpack things really served us. It gave us a process to invest in one another and to value people even when they screwed up. And let's face it, we all screw up and need one another to provide grace when we come to admit our mistakes. Those successful second-chance stories, in which people rise and reinvent themselves, are the stuff of great books.

Mike did those ninety in ninety and the counseling as well. He turned what had become an unmanageable life over to God, lost the excess weight, and gave up the bad nickname. He has been sober for over twenty years, never having relapsed. He became a district manager responsible for nine stores and ran point on strategically shifting managers between stores—air traffic control, as we referred to it—which is one of any company's most arduous tasks. Both his mother and his two sons worked at Malnati's. Mike's wife, Joan, has been a standout support in Buffalo Grove for more than twenty-five years. The Sullivan/Schrager family clearly made a big impact at Malnati's. The restaurant business is a people business, and people will always be human. Extending grace, giving second chances, and challenging people to grow into the best versions of themselves will always be paramount. It's a real cause for celebration when people like Mike seize the opportunity to turn their life around.

Incredible chapters like this would never have happened if Rick and I hadn't experienced what we experienced in our home growing up. That period in our lives led to a need for therapy, and the therapy led to wanting to share what we've learned with our leaders at work. Group provided an opportunity to work through so many issues and see lives changed. It's still amazing to me now to see all the good that has come from what could have been so destructive.

Adding Jimmy, Dennis, and Kathy to my inner circle turned out to be life-giving to me. We grew a trust and a loyalty to one another that took some of the sting out of losing Rick. Along with Stu and Freeland, they wanted to see the company grow. Rick and I were no longer arguing about expansion, and that was liberating.

As the company grew, there were more opportunities for our people to move into management roles. We realized that we had several up-and-coming leaders who were Hispanic. They were well-versed in the operational aspects of our stores, but their limited ability to read and write in English was holding them back from being their most effective when leading teams and dealing with customers. So Jimmy D. and I decided to start another circle that would spend half of our group time in process work, and the other half with each member presenting papers to the group in English. They had assignments like, "What I love about my hometown," or "How I dealt with my last customer service issue." They would write out their report, hand them in for corrections on spelling and grammar, and have a chance to do rewrites. Then they would present the same report orally and receive feedback from the group on their English. It was intense, it made a difference, and most of those individuals stayed with us for the long haul.

Pedro Barrera grew from a busboy who spoke no English to head up all our kitchen operations. He later became our director for new store openings, traveling from store to store to establish standards and to make sure each operation opened with a solid infrastructure. With his vision for finding people larger roles in the company, Pedro has been incredibly influential in helping Hispanics advance within Malnati's, even his siblings Marcela and Felipe.

Everyone has a dream of owning their own home someday. Pedro enlisted my assistance to help some of our most loyal kitchen workers buy homes after they were repeatedly turned down by local banks. I recruited our one-time all-star staff member Marc Miller, who had a mortgage business with his brother. Miller vetted each home that our workers brought to him. When he was satisfied that they had chosen a solid house at a fair price, he wrote their mortgage. We silently guaranteed each of the more than a dozen loans. None of our guys ever missed a payment.

Other key members of that group were Eloy Garcia, who rose from selling Chiclets on the streets of Michoacán to having responsibility for eight to ten stores as a district manager. Hugo Ramos and Nico Garcia both worked their ways up to become GMs of our busiest stores. Jaime Solis is a director of kitchen operations who runs all our festivals and oversees the training around the introduction of new menu items.

Jaime, along with future directors Saul Melchor and Aminadab Reyes, and future district manager Laurynas Brucas, were part of a group of immigrants whom Malnati's sponsored to gain work permits months before the 9/11 attack. In the aftermath of that tragedy, the Department of Homeland Security thoroughly investigated everyone already in the pipeline, and acceptance ground to a snail's pace. It ended up taking eight to ten years, during which time our workers could not leave the United States without having earned work-permit approval. Fortunately, they hung in there, as each one of them went on to play a key role in our company.

Many of these men had two or three other family members join our team along the way. They formed some of the foundational families upon which Malnati's was erected. They became the ones we could point to when we said that we had had the pleasure of watching people grow way past their most outlandish dreams. Not so many years before, Lou had been in virtually the same position as these guys. He loved the idea of America and the chance the country gave to a non-English-speaking, motherless boy from Italy.

These guys and the many Hispanic men and women who followed created some incredible success stories. They only needed a company that believed in them, a little support, and a chance to lead. Some had left their families in Mexico at only fourteen or fifteen years of age, carrying nothing but a dream of finding a job that paid them in dollars. Then they would send most of their earnings home to help support their parents! They'd work jobs as busboys or prep cooks, earn their U.S. citizenship, and pull themselves up into higher-paying roles, all on the strength of their work ethic.

I'm a firm believer in the ability of people. If people are willing to commit their heart and soul to something, if they are willing to do the work to grow themselves, and if they are willing to lean into others around them, there is no telling what they might accomplish. I believe in holding space for future leaders to grow and develop beyond their dreams. Many times, I've had the opportunity to support someone who didn't yet believe in themself, to tell them that I wish they could see themself as I see them, because their potential is so great. Eddie and Peachy had given that kind of support to Rick and me.

People are the key ingredient to success. No one can make it in the restaurant business alone. We have been blessed to be surrounded with the best people you could imagine at Malnati's, and, as the saying goes, it takes a village. The contributions of our team, along with their undying loyalty and passion, stand as the not-so-secret sauce in determining how Lou Malnati's made it successfully to the fifty-year mark.

20.

I loved locating our restaurants in historic structures that we renovated and preserved over time. That spoke to the timelessness of pan pizza as our headliner and to the fact that Malnati is the oldest family name in Chicago pizza. We always thought that giving our stores historical significance helped remind people that we had been around forever, that we were the experts, that Papa and Lou had been there at the conception of pan pizza, and that their family had been preparing it for generations. Our buildings in Schaumburg and Buffalo Grove date to the 1800s, with Lincolnwood, River North, and the store we opened in the basement of the Wrigley Building following close behind. They all have a nostalgic feel, but as anyone who owns an older house knows, a vintage home brings bucketloads of repairs and maintenance.

That's where Funk came in. Larry Funk was my consumer economics teacher (and later, Rick's advisor) in high school. He taught a commonsense curriculum, giving his students pointers on buying a used car, renting your first apartment, or repairing household appliances. Larry didn't believe in wasting things that were still useful, and he could be found in the dumpster at New Trier pulling out computers that had been deemed too old by others. He would repair them and give them to people in need. One time during a restaurant opening, Larry, who was working for us by then, was in the kitchen to check on something when I saw that he was eating a basket of mozzarella sticks, an appetizer we serve. Hungry myself, I asked if I could share one. In tasting it, I found that it was ice cold. I asked him why he was eating cold food. "It wasn't cold when it went into the dining room," he said. I stared at him in awe. Larry's basket had come back from the dining room in a bus pan after a customer hadn't finished it! As I said, he hated to see anything go to waste.

Between his garage and his basement, he had doubles of every tool ever made, along with parts for clocks. And not just any clocks. Larry had coauthored books on clocks and amassed one of the largest collections of grandfather and swinging ball clocks in the country. He always had the parts of two or three splayed across the workbench in his basement. If you had the time, he loved to talk you through what made them tick.

Our old buildings needed TLC and regular repairs, and Funk was just the guy to do it. Not long after our dad died, he started helping part-time while he was still teaching, but his part-time was like any normal person's full-time. He had more energy than any human being I'd ever met and could seemingly go for three or four days without sleep. He preferred working through the night, because there would be no one around to bother him. He and his wife, Barbara, had no children, and like Peachy and Eddie Lis, they sort of adopted Rick and me as their kids.

By the time we opened the twelfth or thirteenth store, there weren't enough hours in the day for Larry to both teach and manage our construction and maintenance. We asked him to quit teaching, and though he was close to earning a full pension, he agreed. I think that having known Lou and having watched his former students lose their dad at such a young age, he generously offered himself up to do anything in his power to help us succeed.

One Thanksgiving weekend in 1998, our Schaumburg kitchen crew was doing a deep clean and accidentally ripped a gas hose out of its wall connection, igniting a terrible fire in the vintage building. Larry led a massive rebuild that included replacing all the HVAC ductwork, bringing in a new electrical service, refacing the kitchen and the bar, and trading out every piece of kitchen equipment due to smoke damage.

In a preliminary inspection after the fire, our insurance company told us it would take a minimum of three to four months to get the place back in shape to reopen. Larry completed the total renovation in seventeen days, during which time he only left the store twice. He slept in the basement storage area for a few hours each night as he supervised crews working around the clock. His primary concern was for our Schaumburg team and making sure they could return to work for the busy Christmas holiday season. That example was typical—he regularly did things in a time frame that should not have been humanly possible. Larry held himself to high standards and a tight schedule because he cared so deeply for us and for our Malnati community.

He took on another crazy and highly technical project in our River North store. In that building we had had to locate our kitchen in the basement in order to allow for enough seats in the first-floor dining room. But there were repeated plumbing issues. On top of that, we were in one of those age old structures where the basement had been the original first floor, so the foundation was atypical. Intricate ceramic tile work surrounded the opening in the vault under the sidewalk, the entrance to the building one hundred years ago. In the aftermath of the Great Chicago Fire in 1871, the street had been raised a full ten feet to make space to install underground plumbing throughout the neighborhood. I had always wondered why ruins in Rome were discovered beneath the existing city, and this helped me begin to understand.

Larry assembled a crew of contractors who relished a challenge. They dug deeper in the basement, which, because of ductwork and overhead plumbing, had only a five-foot-ten-inch head clearance in some places. Larry and his crew worked like in the days of the pharaoh, carrying dirt and chunks of concrete out in pails around the clock; they finished in two weeks. The hope was to fix the leaks and make enough room to give us more volume of air movement, to make some of Chicago's ridiculously hot summer days feel like only ninety-five degrees, not 195! Led by Larry's contagious energy, the project gave us the ability to grow this little store in River North into one of the strongest producers in the company.

21.

Toward the end of the rebuilding of the kitchen at River North, one of our leaders taught me a lesson in people management that I'll never forget. Lynn Young was the GM of River North when Larry Funk tore the place up that winter. I had hired Lynn after David Eisenberg, our oven repair guru, recommended a woman who he said was on top of every detail for a group of Burger Kings owned by a local franchisee. She walked in for the interview in a full-length fur coat. Burger King must pay a lot better than we do, I thought to myself.

She and I talked for at least two hours, as she told me story after story about what she had witnessed and managed through while overseeing multiple locations in the rough part of Chicago's South Side. She spoke about setting traps and catching would-be thieves who worked in her stores. She spoke of homeless people who were convinced that Burger King was their home address. She shared lessons she had learned from her penny-pinching boss, who had built a profitable business through threats and instilling the fear of God in his people. Lynn had received a unique education.

Jimmy D. always talked about the difference between GMs who know how to make money and those who do not. The ones who do are meticulous about planning ahead. Managing our cost of labor is where a great manager separates herself from others, because that is the single cost that can make or break us. Great managers aren't sticklers for people punching out right when the schedule dictates or for rarely paying overtime in their store. Their labor cost is good because they typically don't have to ramp up by adding more people for bigger sales days. They simply have a solid, loyal, veteran crew who can stretch themselves to work like two or three people during crunch time.

Hospitality is king, but making money is also important, so having managers who know how to bring in the profits is crucial to ongoing success.

As this story goes, while Funk was wrapping up the new, rebuilt basement kitchen, I was getting frustrated that our people weren't capturing my vision for the dining room. I wanted the customers to see a space that appeared as shiny and fresh as the new kitchen. There was construction dust everywhere, but our staff seemed overwhelmed and content to replace the tables and chairs where they belonged and reopen the doors. I barked to no one in particular, "It's not only what you can see, but be proud enough to clean what you can't see as well!" Then I got down on my back and ferociously chiseled gum off the underside of one of the booths, trying to make a point to anyone who might notice.

After about a half hour of grumbling and picking at remnants of OPG (other people's gum) I jumped up to see what the staff was doing. Why weren't they on the ground following my friendly example? I rumbled out of the dining room and into the bar area and found Lynn perched atop the bar, where she could see the entire room. From there, she oversaw a handful of operations. She shouted to two kids cleaning the front windows to use newspaper, not paper towels. She coached three men on all fours scrubbing the hard-to-access parts of the railings that separate the eating space from the waiting space. She turned from that group to the people scrubbing out the beer coolers and crawling under the bar sinks, coming face to face with the "bar cheese" (not an appetizer!) that had recently accumulated. "Get hotter water! Hold your nose!" she cried.

As I studied what was going on, Lynn never lifted a finger. She just kept spinning and barking new orders, as the room was quickly coming together. Each of the dozen or so people she was commandeering was fully focused and engaged in what they were doing. I had an epiphany: My grousing and pounding on the underside of tables hadn't moved the needle much in the dining room. But Lynn was tuned into every single person in that bar and was getting big results—the epitome of a great manager.

In watching Lynn, I realized that great managers find the spot where they can be in the middle of the action and manage from there. I'm talking here about the restaurant business, but the lessons apply to almost all kinds of enterprises. Be the conductor of the orchestra and let members of your team play their roles; don't try to do it yourself, like me. Too many of us think we're helping when we pigeonhole ourselves into a role in the kitchen. We can pat dough or prep sausage pizzas quickly or jump over to the table where carryout pizzas are flipped from pans into boxes. But those sorts of "head down" roles—while they may help momentarily and may even prove to you and your team that you're someone willing to get down and dirty—don't amount to managing.

A manager needs to have their head on a swivel, seeing and hearing everything, giving directions and corrections to their domain. A great manager is always teaching, always encouraging, always knowing where to focus their attention. They must be everywhere at once, know precisely what each member of their crew should be doing at any given moment. They must train their team to see their store exactly as the customer will see it, but at least a moment before, so they can make sure the gum wrapper is picked right up, the chairs are rubbed clean, and the tabletop has been wiped, dried, and organized just before the guest approaches. They have to know if the wings are hot, the salad cold, and the pizza on time; and they have to make sure the check is delivered, payment collected, and our guests graciously thanked for choosing Lou's tonight.

A great GM takes ownership. I like to listen for how a GM talks about their store and their people. I look for how they hold the store. When they refer to it, it needs to be "my store" and not "the store." When a mistake is made, I want to see them take responsibility. When a milestone is achieved, I want them to hold it with personal pride. I want to hear a GM bragging about their store. I want to both hear and feel their swagger when they speak. That's when I know that the right attachment has been made between GM and restaurant, and that I can trust them to treat our business as their own. Then I can sleep at night.

22.

THE YEAR 2004 WAS A banner year for Malnati's. Revenue was up and to the right in all our stores, and we were building momentum. We had finally outgrown our shoebox office above the Lincolnwood restaurant and relocated to Northbrook, where we had more office space for our support services people, as well as a warehouse for our Tastes of Chicago shipping business. But before we hit the gas, we knew we needed to make two more great hires to fill out our strategic leadership team in the areas of human resources and marketing.

Gabriella Streicher was an attorney who preferred HR to law, and she quickly brought best practices to our company. I'm sure she initially saw us as a bunch of cowboys who had few rules and didn't much like to keep records. She set out to protect us from ourselves and create consistencies for handling staff issues from store to store.

By then, with more than twenty-five locations, inconsistency was the only thing that was truly predictable. Inconsistency in our food was always top of mind, and we knew that if we allowed that to happen, it would ruin us. But inconsistency in giving raises, in hiring and training staff—those things can create a slow but painful death as well. Gabriella moved us out of the dark ages.

Internally, she and Stu worked together with our ops team to create a farm system that identified staff members who had leadership potential so that we could maximize their training by beginning before there was an actual need. That made their eventual transition into management smoother. Gabriella rewrote company rules and guidelines to provide far greater clarity than what existed. She created standards for the way managers were to mete out discipline to staffers who failed to comply with policy so that consequences were undeviating from store to store.

Gabriella was reluctant to buy into Group at first. Experience had taught her that sharing her feelings with coworkers, especially with her superiors, was ill-advised. In her past employment, she had been hurt because of her openness, and she wasn't in a hurry to make that mistake again. But after watching other leaders at Malnati's experience growth by being open to their colleagues' feedback, she changed her mind and leaned into the circle. In later years, she would go on to take charge of the oversight of Group experience in the company.

In the marketing department, Mindy LaFlamme took over after an eighteen-year stint with the Chicago region's urban transportation system, the RTA. I got a call from David Kaplan, a longtime friend and the sports anchor at WGN, Chicago's most prominent radio station at the time. He had heard that we were searching for a marketing director and asked if I would interview the woman he was about to marry. I was terribly reluctant—I dreaded having to reject her and thus potentially harm my relationship with Kap. The company advertised on WGN regularly and he was a great promoter of Malnati's. Marketing director was a senior role, and I couldn't even consider bringing in someone incapable as a favor to a friend.

After Kaplan's third call, I finally had someone meet Mindy with the secret agenda to persuade her to pursue a job elsewhere. But the report on her interview came back glowing, and then Stu met with her, and he was thumbs up as well. Finally, I agreed to have a conversation with Mindy. Immediately, I was impressed by her unassuming manner, and I liked the practical, get-in-the-trenches approach she took to marketing. We desperately needed someone who could take Malnati's to a new level, and she seemed to believe that a solid work ethic was vital, just as we did.

Mindy turned things upside down in marketing and made everything better. She improved our branding, our public relations, and she designed a grassroots approach to garner attention for each store in its individual market. Mindy is a type A personality on steroids. A typical day saw her working out for an hour before six a.m., getting into the office early, holding five or six meetings with team members, jumping on the assembly line with our Tastes of Chicago crew to make sure all the packages got out, cooking dinner for her three boys and her new husband, Kap, pitching on her softball team, then staying up until two a.m., tending to the work she brought home while baking cookies for a Malnati team member's birthday. She easily set the bar for discipline in the company, as others marveled at how she continued to perform like that week after week.

Lou had passed on a model for creating awareness of Malnati's by doing good in the community. He didn't like to spend money on advertising and would rather stay in his sweet spot by putting together an event like his tribute to Brian Piccolo, where he could use his resources to produce positive outcomes. Over more than fifty years, the fundraiser that Lou and Jean first hosted in Lincolnwood in 1971 has morphed slightly, and what is now referred to as The Lou Malnati Cancer Benefit has gone on to raise millions of dollars toward the cause of cancer research and support for cancer victims. My mom chairs the twenty-person board that hosts the dinner and auction, and Mindy brought her energy to this annual event and proceeded to take it to a whole new level.

One of our finest moments in marketing Malnati's came when we received an invitation to appear on *The Daily Show with Jon Stewart*. The coup developed in November 2013 after Chicago Mayor Rahm Emanuel contended with New York Mayor Michael Bloomberg over which city could boast the tallest building in the country. Jon Stewart picked up on the childishness of the controversy and began mocking everything Chicago, especially deep-dish pizza. He had the nerve to call it "tomato soup in a bread bowl"! At the time, Jeanne and I happened to be in NYC visiting Will, so the plan was for the three of us to collaborate on our own video rebuttal to Stewart's abuse of Chicago.

In the video, I played the part of a frustrated Chicago Pizza Man who was upset about Stewart's poor depiction of my hometown and decided to fly to the Big Apple to see if things in New York City actually were better than things in Chicago. We filmed at Freedom Tower (One World Trade Center) on a very cloudy day, when we could only see the lower twenty floors, but we pressed ahead in a tongue-in-cheek sort of way and maintained that our Chicago mayor was right! The grand NY structure "clearly appeared" to be six to eight inches shorter than Chicago's Willis Tower (the former Sears Tower).

Our next stop was at a corner pizza joint in the Chelsea neighborhood. I tried to take a bite of a slice of New York thin-crust, and it flopped over. Limp. I gave it another chance. This time the entire layer of cheese slid off as I attempted to eat it. "Big Apple, little pizza!" I declared.

Finally, Jeanne, Will, and I stopped in front of Stewart's studio on Sunday morning, and, of course, nobody answered when I rang the bell. I set one of our Tastes of Chicago frozen pizzas on the doorstep and left a note asking Stewart to call me. On the video, I told him I'd fly back and make some real Chicago pizza, and he could invite his friends, too.

Then our marketing team took over. Led by Mindy and her assistant, Meggie Lindberg, they figured out how to press the right buttons to have the video go viral, and overnight it garnered over a million views. Stewart's producer noticed, and we were invited onto the show the next night. Mindy hopped on an airplane and flew to New York with a suitcase full of fresh ingredients, and I used the kitchen of a local pizzeria to cook deep-dish from scratch so that we could have Stewart taste it on the show.

About an hour before we went on the air, I met Stewart. He was warm and affable. He reassured me that we were filming the show hours before it would air. Even though he had a live studio audience, if we didn't like how our segment went, we could always do a retake. That made me slightly less anxious until just before I was to walk out on stage and I asked Stewart's producer how often they redo segments like mine. "I've been here nine years, and we've never done that," he said.

Just then I heard Stewart introduce me, and the producer pushed me out, deep-dish in hand, to greet the host at his interview desk. Better not blow it! Stewart had decided that our backstage prep conversation, in which we had discussed how the two of us would reestablish the broken peace between Chicago and New York, went well. Well enough that he decided I didn't need to read from the cue cards that his staff had prepared. The cue cards were gone as I walked out there into the glare of the bright lights, and I was wondering if he had made a big mistake.

We poked fun at each other for a few minutes. Stewart pretended that the slice of Malnati's pizza that I fed him was so heavy he couldn't pick it up. He acted offended when I suggested that he sample it with a knife and fork instead of picking it up in his hands. But when he tasted it, he loved it, and he proposed a truce. Finally, we both agreed to disagree about whose pizza was best, but we were in lockstep in our mutual belief that California pizza is simply awful.

In attempting to settle the long-standing pizza war between New York and Chicago, we made a slew of new fans. In the two days following the show, we would see an additional $300,000 in e-commerce orders through Tastes of Chicago from all over the country, and a giant sales spike in our stores in Chicago from people who watched the show. Mindy and her team had succeeded in seizing the moment and creating an indelible pizza memory in the minds of countless Americans.

23.

In 2006, Stu and I came to believe we could have success opening a restaurant in the far northwest suburbs. Randall Road had become a main north-south artery, and the area around Crystal Lake and Algonquin had seen record growth and was poised for more. Lower land costs in the early 2000s spurred contractors, who could build bigger homes at half the price. We scoured the area every chance we got, always looking for shuttered restaurants that we could make over. We never found any, and that was good and bad. Good because existing businesses were successful. Bad because building a restaurant from the ground up was something we had not done before, and we knew it would be far more expensive.

My friend Brett Lundstrom finally discovered a ten-acre piece of land in the tiny community of Lakewood, slightly west of Randall Road and Crystal Lake and adjacent to the towns of Huntley and Lake in the Hills. Fewer than five thousand people reside in Lakewood. None of these towns alone has an adequate population to support a restaurant, but grouped together, more than one hundred thousand people lived in the area, and we were convinced a Malnati's could thrive. Brett became our partner in the real estate deal after we had carved out two acres for our restaurant. We decided to build a retail strip center next to the free-standing restaurant, because even though these would be the first businesses established in Lakewood, the area had affluence, and we believed that Malnati's would draw enough attention to convince other retailers to place stores there as well.

The site was quite rural, and we discovered the ruined foundation of what appeared to be an old silo on the property. Wanting to build a structure to echo what might have been there before, we chose a country barn theme. We drove around the area looking at existing barns, trying to draw inspiration. We decided we would erect a big, round silo out of fieldstone as the focal point. It would become a private room housing a big round table for twelve with a lazy Susan in the center. The kitchen, bar, and dining rooms behind it were of cedar and were painted barn red.

Once we had finalized the purchase of the property and knew how we wanted the place to look and feel, Jeanne and I went to work locating the accoutrements that would be necessary to create a homey, farm-like atmosphere. Because getting zoning approvals and building the restaurant was not a quick process, we had a little over a year to be on the hunt for ideas and to assemble a large collection of farm implements.

We loved how farmers often created a tractor graveyard of sorts, where Ol' Betsy was retired to somewhere on the front of their property where they could celebrate her fine career and allow her to spend eternity slowly developing that perfect, rustic, aged look. So we located a dead tractor of our own and rolled it into the landscape in front of the silo. We found a tiller, old metal chairs, vintage ten-gallon milk cans, wooden milk churns, and an old double wash basin. We either planted flowers in the old items or just laid them among the wildflowers and sweet grass that was growing tall. All the stuff that a farm family would have used and randomly left lying around the property would be there to welcome our new guests to Lakewood.

Inside, the restaurant was colorful and whimsical. Bright farm scenes painted in chalk on black tar paper were the work of famous downstate

Illinois artist George Colin. We hung folk art farm-stand signs hawking eggs, corn, and fresh berries and decorated with large farm tools, including sickles, scythes, and a bull castrator. One long wall boasted a collage fashioned of vintage doors and shutters that had fallen off their homes years ago. On smaller walls, Jeanne built collections of old painted gadgets and contrivances, some walls with only green items, some with only yellow. The highlight of the front dining room was a 10,000-gallon bucket of Lou Malnati's California plum tomatoes.

The back dining room abutted a pond and the edge of the twelfth hole of RedTail Golf Course. Large windows offered diners a chance to be entertained by errant tee shots hit by local hackers. It took some of the golfers a while to notice that a new restaurant had opened. Many were caught in the indiscretion of relieving their bladders in a previously private area behind the tee, a space now confronting the picture window where families dined at Malnati's.

As with many of our large openings, due to Jeanne's ability to be flexible with her client schedule, she was willing to move to the area for six months so I wouldn't have to worry about a daily drive to and from the new store, which was a full hour away from our home. Brett and his wife, Rachel, owned a vacant house only a couple miles away and graciously made it available to us. Will joined us there as well.

After wearying of his Manhattan nightclub job, he had come back to Chicago to help with Lakewood. Again, our hopes were raised, as we assumed Will would stay on, join Malnati's permanently, and extend our lineage into the next generation. He jumped right in and worked his butt off—especially in the kitchen—and was welcomed by everyone. He had learned much in the few years that he managed the clubs in New York, and I was impressed with his leadership and his ability to motivate the people around him. I was equally impressed with his willingness to pick up a mop and do the dirty work along with his team when it was necessary.

After several months, Will returned to NYC to pack up his apartment and prepare to move back to Chicago for good. But Jeanne and

I were in bed one night when Will called us late, needing to talk. He explained that he had spent some time with a few of his closest friends in New York, and he was confused about what he really wanted to do. He pointed out that he had built up a large book of important contacts— people in New York who were movers and shakers. He felt that if he was ever to try to venture out on his own in the restaurant business in the Big Apple, the time would be now, while his book was fresh.

I listened in disbelief. I had assumed that had he returned to Chicago as planned, he would succeed me someday at the helm of his family's flourishing company. We would get to work side by side, and I'd teach him everything I knew. How was that not his best option? Why would he choose to do something on his own when we could do something together? I did not understand. I was way easier to work with than Lou would have been, right?

Jeanne was able to love Will right where he was. Moms will always support their kids, no matter what happens. She told him to follow his heart, but mine was crushed. That completed the hat trick for me. My dad had died, then my brother had left to coach, and now my son was choosing to work in the same business as I, but not with me in Chicago. The three men in my life had all left me.

24.

IN THE EARLY FALL OF 2008, we were contacted by the Food Network to participate in a new show titled *Pie Nation*. The show would highlight the best pizzas in the country, and they wanted to showcase Lou Malnati's on their inaugural broadcast. I had heard a little about the Food Network, but the channel wasn't on our regular TV rotation at home. The producers told our marketing department that I'd need to block out two entire days in September for filming. I pushed back. Two days? Could a show on Food Network draw a large enough audience to be worth that kind of time investment?

I ended up being more than pleasantly surprised. I first met the modest film crew of two people and a producer at Millennium Park in front of Cloud Gate, the sculpture widely known as the Bean. The artist Anish Kapoor had built the 110-ton, 66-foot-long, and 33-foot-high stainless-steel structure for the opening of the new park in 2004. One of the world's largest outdoor works of interactive art, the Bean allows people to be photographed in front of a reflection of the beautiful Chicago skyline. The sculpture is one of the city's biggest tourist draws. We did several promotional takes there for the debut of *Pie Nation* and then headed to nearby Soldier Field, the stadium where the Chicago Bears play.

We were filming on a Monday in September, and the Bears were preparing to host *Monday Night Football* that evening. Rabid fans had begun tailgating early that morning, and as we waded into the parking lot on the south side of the stadium, all I could smell was meat. Seasoned tailgate veterans were showing off their talents, grilling brats and sausages, burgers and steaks. Music blared, people sang the century-old Bears theme song, and everyone was outfitted in Bears jerseys or Mike Ditka sweaters, or costumed to look like Bill Swerski's Superfans from the popular *SNL* sketch that immortalized the expression "da Bears." The TV crew loved capturing the absurdity of the crazed Bears audience as a backdrop for me preparing Malnati's deep-dish pizza from scratch in the middle of the giant parking lot.

The next morning, I met the film crew in Buffalo Grove. When I pulled up to the store, I was amazed that they had basically taken over the entire property. The tables had all been cleared out of our main dining room, and they had lighting and boom microphones arranged to completely cover the area. Painted in colored chalk on the asphalt in front of our entrance was a twelve-foot round drawing of the world. In the center was North America and in the heart of the U.S. was a banner that read "Pie Nation." Yesterday's modest crew had expanded explosively. There had to be twenty people scurrying around, setting up for today's filming. My initial skepticism had disappeared, as I realized that the Food Network had a king-size budget for this new show.

The producers had seduced 150 or so of our best customers to come and serve as the audience. I was asked to stand behind a makeshift prep table at one end of the dining room and slowly explain to the crowd a little about each ingredient that goes into the creation of our pizza. The cameras were rolling and the lights were bright as I prepared a pizza while simultaneously sharing some of our secrets about how long we allow our dough to rest, how the diet of the Wisconsin dairy cows affects our mozzarella, and what we demand from a tomato crop. When

I finished, they asked me to walk through the whole process again. I presumed they wanted extra footage.

Having already used my best material (OK, my only material) to entertain the crowd, I scrambled to come up with something fresh and semi-enlightening to say, lest I embarrass myself in front of a big group of Lou Malnati disciples. Then, just before I was about to start tripping over my own words, a guy walked in from the back of the room, and immediately the spectators began to whisper and ogle. Next, they began to cheer. I panicked. Although I'm not the sharpest tool in the shed, I quickly realized that I was supposed to recognize the young, confident man striding toward me. But I didn't have the faintest idea who he was. I improvised with a broad smile and my best phony greeting, "Heyyyy . . . it's you! Welcome!" Jeanne was just offstage, and I desperately whispered, "Find out who this guy is!" She polled a group of onlookers, and someone told her it was Bobby Flay, the famous New York chef and Emmy Award–winning poster boy for the Food Network. He walked up, introduced himself, and boldly asked, "Are you ready for a Pizza Throwdown?"

The whole *Pie Nation* concept had been a ruse to lull me into a state of confidence before Flay would appear and challenge me to a cooking contest. As I learned later, week in and week out, the show would come up with clever ways to surprise restaurateurs across America, and then battle test their specialty against the kitchen acumen of Flay and his team. This week, he and his sous chefs were trying to strut into my backyard and make a tastier pan pizza than I do. The show, *Throwdown with Bobby Flay*, had been going since 2006 and was a Food Network hit.

Over the course of nine seasons, this was the only episode Flay would film in Chicago. As was typical of the series, local judges were selected to decide the contest. For our event, the officials were Pat Bruno, longtime food writer for the *Chicago Sun-Times*, and Glen Kozlowski, a talk show host and former Chicago Bear. For his entry, Flay chose to go for extravagance, cooking up spicy sausage, fontina cheese, and broccoli rabe. Me? I just rode our Chicago Classic—cheese and sausage with butter crust—all the way to the bank. I also wielded a secret weapon: Pedro Barrera in the kitchen making sure that each of our pizzas was engineered to perfection.

Both judges crowned Lou Malnati's Throwdown champ that day to the roaring delight of the audience. As we tuned in to watch the show when it aired a few weeks later, and then noticed that Food Network replayed it at least a few dozen more times, all we could think about was how grateful we were that we won. With the number of texts and social media mentions we received after each rerun, can you imagine what it would have felt like to watch us lose time after time?

25.

Shortly after I read Jim Collins's book *Good to Great*, I wanted to apply his research on what separated average companies from those that went on to become best in class. At a team meeting, I quoted Collins and said I thought we had all the right people on the bus, a factor far more important than which seat any of us occupied. If we were all willing to wear several hats instead of siloing ourselves away, we had a chance to have a great run. A team that looks to pitch in wherever and whenever necessary is a team that wins. At the end of that meeting, we all agreed that a critical piece of our growth agenda should be for us to take on and eventually dominate Chicago's downtown pizza scene.

Chicago's business and hotel district was flourishing under the leadership of Mayor Richard M. Daley. The opening of Millennium Park in 2004 and the added emphasis on the Bureau of Tourism began to attract increasing numbers of world travelers to the Windy City. Given that we had the best pizza and the oldest name in Chicago pizza, we figured that becoming the main player in the city center was part of our birthright. And since we now had the organization that could execute a plan, we set out to make Malnati's the cornerstone of all things pizza in Chicago. We didn't want anyone to start a conversation about Chicago pizza without naming Lou Malnati's in their first breath.

Over the first decade or so of the twenty-first century, we basically doubled the size of our company and planted our flag firmly in the city proper. As the Great Recession of 2007–2009 set in and giant investment banks such as Bear Stearns and Lehman Brothers went under, we theorized that even though our business was also fighting through this crisis, this would be the perfect time to strike a below-market deal for a store in Chicago's Gold Coast, the affluent neighborhood along the lake and just north of the Loop. Gold Coast landlords had been able to garner rents of $75–100 per square foot before the recession, but suddenly retailers had tightened expenses and taken a break from opening new stores. If we were willing to take a risk that the world would soon reset itself, we could enter a neighborhood that previously had been out of our reach financially for less than $35 per square foot!

We jumped at an opportunity to locate in the spot that the upscale clothing store Anthropologie was exiting at 1120 North State Street, in a building that was owned by one of my first-grade classmates, David Blum. David leased us 10,000 square feet just off the famed Viagra Triangle, the Gold Coast intersection anchored by Gibsons Steakhouse and known for the well-heeled older men and much younger women who frequent the local bars. The lively nighttime activity made our new location a popular site for Chicagoans who lived in the nearby lakefront condos, as well as the tourists who filled the many area hotels.

At the same time that we put three hundred seats into 1120 North State Street, we added a hundred in an expansion of our South Loop facility. Soon after, we purchased the building that housed our River North store and added 125 seats, and then bought a two-hundred-seat West Loop store from fabled chef Ina Pinkney, who was looking to retire. The coup de grâce came in 2019, when we leased the basement of one of Chicago's most recognizable landmarks, the Wrigley Building, which sits at Michigan Avenue and the Chicago River (Main & Main). Those five stores made it a fait accompli that anyone and everyone who was visiting the pizza capital of the world to sample their first pan pizza would find a Lou Malnati's in proximity. Lou would have absolutely loved it! He owned downtown. Again!

Years had passed since he had thought better of opening down the street from Uno and Due and went to the suburbs instead. Years since the thirty-nine-year-old restaurant manager had dared to ask Ike Sewell if the fabled pizzerias might someday become his. And now that dream had come full circle, and Lou Malnati's banner held prominence across the Chicago skyline. Earlier, we had built a stronghold in Chicago's north and northwest suburbs, but we never attracted a national level of attention and recognizability until we invaded downtown. The volume of visitors that the city has continued to attract, and the fact that so many of them venture into one of our downtown stores, has served to spread Lou's legend throughout the country and around the world.

I loved it when a local fellow named Jonathan Porter started Chicago Pizza Tours, an attraction that would take visitors to Malnati's, as well as to the original Pizzeria Uno and other pizzerias to sample and compare institutions, some of which had stood for fifty years or more. Hey, I like to sample and compare myself. I'm fine with people trying everyone else's food, as long as they get to try ours.

As far as our deep-dish competitors were concerned, I grew up regarding Uno as the mecca of pizzadom. Still, Uno's pizza is not quite as it used to be—the ownership group that bought the operation from Ike Sewell changed the pizza radically in the 1980s as they sped up the cooking process. At one point, they went so far as to take "pizzeria" out of the restaurant's name. But I still had memories of visiting my dad and my grandfather there as a young boy, and all the youthful wonder and pleasures would rush back when Jeanne and I stopped by incognito when we celebrated our anniversary with a staycation weekend in the city.

Our historic rivals include Gino's East, with its yellow cornmeal crust developed by Alice Redmond, the cook basically kidnapped from

Uno by Gino's owners, two former cab drivers. And then there is Giordano's, offering a pizza that stuffs all the ingredients between two layers of dough.

All these pizzas have their followings and add to the fascination with Chicago pizza. But if you laid them all out for a taste test, I'm betting we would come out the hands-down winner. In 2010, we actually faced off against Uno on the cable TV show *Food Wars* and were the overwhelming favorite of the judges.

In 2012, we competed against Giordano's on *Steve Harvey*. Both rivals were to prepare enough pizza for the members of the studio audience to taste live on the show. The hundred or so people would then vote for the one they preferred and thus ordain the winner of the Golden Fork Trophy. Giordano's has a restaurant next door to Harvey's TV studio at the NBC Tower, so staffers prepared a big stack of pizzas in their nearby kitchen and a delivery guy walked them over. The nearest Malnati's was at least a mile away. So we dropped one of our 1,500-pound Blodgett oven stacks and a five-foot-tall cylinder of propane gas on the sidewalk of Lower Michigan Avenue, directly underneath NBC. This way, our pizzas would be as fresh as any you would eat in one of our stores.

When it was time to feed the audience, we ran the pizzas upstairs and quickly plated them to send into the small auditorium. Giordano's did the same. After the votes were compiled, Steve Harvey announced that Malnati's had won by a sliver, and he presented me the coveted trophy that sits proudly today on the back bar of our Gold Coast store.

A few hours after we finished taping the show, Steve called and told me he thought our pizza was so good that he wanted to bring his wife and family in for dinner that night. When I met them, I asked Steve if we had really just won by "a sliver." He confided that we had actually won by a landslide, but he couldn't say that on TV or other restaurateurs would be afraid to compete for fear of embarrassment!

Of course there have always been other styles of pizza in Chicagoland. Thin crust pizza has a strong following on the South and Southwest sides of town. Some people search out a good Neapolitan pie. I'm a big fan of Spacca Napoli. But the pan pizza that was first served at Pizzeria Uno and then perfected at Lou Malnati's has become the treasured choice and the pizza darling of Chicagoans.

When food writer Steve Dolinsky made the uninformed, headline-seeking suggestion that "tavern-style pizza" was perhaps the pick of most true Chicagoans, I responded quickly, asking for his data. Then I showed him that in 2020, Malnati's sold 6.2 million pizzas in the Chicago area. If we take away the eight hundred thousand that were sold in our five downtown restaurants (because he claimed that only tourists ate there, which is not even remotely true), we're at 5.4 million pizzas. About 1.5 million of the pizzas we sell are our own fabulous thin-crust variety. Doing the math, that still leaves us with about four million Malnati's pan pizzas consumed annually by Chicagoans in Chicagoland. Trust me when I say that no Chicago pizzeria sells four million tavern-style pizzas annually. Not even close! Add sales at all the pizzerias together, and I still don't think it's close. I think the data would show that Chicagoans buy deep-dish about two-to-one over thin pizza. I'm still waiting for Steve Dolinsky to retract his statement, because those were fighting words!

And hold on! I'm not done yet with this rant.

I am sick of writers using their pulpit to disparage deep-dish pizza. They are wanting to make a name for themselves, so they try to get people's attention by being a contrarian. Pay no mind to the fact that Chicagoans prefer deep-dish to thin-crust and always have. Equally frustrating are the promoters who try to create a nuanced category that doesn't even exist, such as so-called tavern-style pizza. I asked Nick Perrino of Home Run Inn if he makes thin-crust or tavern-style. "I'm not sure what tavern-style even means," he said. "I think it's a new marketing catchphrase." And Nick's great-grandfather started making his pizza seventy-five years ago in a tavern. Uno and Due were nothing more than taverns that sold pizza. Maybe we should be calling deep-dish tavern-style!

I'm a lover of pizza. Deep-dish, thin-crust, Neapolitan, purple, green . . . I will try anything. My preference is deep-dish, because I think it most embodies what any great meal should be: It's delicious, it's something I dream about both before and after I eat it, and there's enough to feed me and my family. While other styles of pizza are often good, ask yourself if the pizza was memorable, or if it was just a bridge to your next meal. You'll never say that about deep-dish.

When a writer criticizes deep-dish, I take it personally. I've been in this business full-time for forty-four years now, and for six years before that when I was a kid in school. My father and his father before him made deep-dish pizza here for their entire careers. Malnati's represents around 3,500 staff members today, people who collectively pour all their energy into creating a product that Chicago has been proud to call its own since the 1940s.

The city and its residents know what they love—and it's been Malnati's pizza for half a century.

26.

Mark Agnew was a student-athlete whom Rick had introduced me to when he started coaching at New Trier in the mid-1990s. I recall playing basketball in some off-season pickup games with Mark and several members of Rick's team. I was clearly filler, out there to get in a good run, while Mark could hold his own with the best players in the school, though he wasn't on the basketball team. He was the starting quarterback for the football team, and surely among the top two or three athletes in a school of three thousand kids.

While at New Trier, Rick started Fellowship of Christian Athletes gatherings that were held at the Agnew home. The setting was helpful in attracting students, because Mark became friends with everyone who crossed his path. He had that level of magnetism, the ability to relate to people on almost any topic, and a laugh that would win you over and leave you wanting more. One time he told me that he had about thirty BFFs, and while that sounds ridiculous, I'm sure that if you polled people who know Mark and asked them about their relationship, at least double that number would claim he was their closest friend in the world.

Mark attended the School of Hotel Administration at Cornell and then earned an MBA from the University of Chicago. At each stop,

Malnati's played a role in his advancement. He did an internship at our Buffalo Grove store during college, and during grad school he brought in a team of four to do an in-depth study of our e-commerce business. After U of C, he learned investment banking at Deutsche Bank and then joined the private equity firm of Dixon Midland. With the 2007–09 recession, his partners decided to slow the deal flow. Mark stayed for a while and then decided he would go out on his own. He approached me as a potential investor in a business he was looking to buy and operate in Ohio.

A month or two later, I asked for an update on his potential opportunity and told him I'd meet him at Walker Brothers Original Pancake House in Glenview, my go-to breakfast meeting spot. Not because it's close to our home, but because the thought of having French crêpes with fresh strawberries and that decadent orange sauce cranks me up! The excitement about eating my favorite foods can build for days. Food has always been my love language. But I digress . . .

When we met, Mark was in a good mood, as always, and our twenty-year age difference never mattered, as we easily connected and enjoyed one another's company. He told me that it looked as if his deal in Ohio was cratering. He was sad, as he had put a ton of time into trying to make it work, but as was typical of Mark, he said, "It just wasn't meant to be, and I'm OK with that."

I figured his plan would be to pursue another position in private equity or some other business you read about in *Barron's*, but with more than moderate trepidation, I asked, "What would you think about joining us at Malnati's?"

He broke into a gigantic smile. "Are you kidding?" he said. "That would be my dream job! There's nowhere I'd rather be."

I'd always believed that the restaurant business was a young person's business, and at fifty-six, I was running out of daylight. The pace is too fast and the operation too demanding of both time and energy. Eventually, that catches up with all of us. Bringing on Mark in 2011 gave me a second wind. A personality profiler predicted that Mark and I would spur each other on, and together ignite welcome expansion. The profiler actually said that "we'd be like matches and gasoline," which I interpreted in a positive light.

Though Mark had an MBA and ten years of experience in private equity, he agreed to invest months in training in multiple stores, learning the ins and outs of how our kitchens operated and how we went overboard for our guests. He did ride-alongs with our district managers, gaining their insights and developing a real understanding of the complexity of their jobs. He earned credibility with our longtime staff members, because after he had worked a shift with them, they felt as if they knew him; that helped make them more accepting of changes he would later initiate.

During the seven years of Mark's involvement, we continued to grow sales and increase profitability in all our stores. Our EBITDA (earnings before interest, taxes, depreciation, and amortization) grew from $8 million to $20 million a year. Mark hired Ben Beckstrom as our chief information officer, and together they led us into online ordering and the information age well before most other operators figured out that online ordering would be critical for the future. One minute we were adding phone lines to capture our customer orders, and the next we were eliminating phone worker positions because people were ready to order online. Mark knew that information technology would become central to everything we did.

He became president in 2013, and Stu Cohen, who had been president, adopted the vice chairman role. As in many power exchanges, Mark was eager to advance and felt that he was ready to be handed the reins of the company before Stu was ready to get off the horse. Stu could see that the younger leader would play a key role in Malnati's future, but also felt that at fifty-eight years old, he was still in his prime. Also, when Mark signed on, I had told Stu that it would be three years before we elevated Mark, and we hadn't quite reached the two-year mark. In my experience, transitions like these almost never happen easefully, and they tend to go worse when someone like me decides to change the schedule. Malnati's was enjoying some of our best years since the expansion had begun in the downtown market, and Stu, as always, was doing a great job. But ultimately, I chose to move Mark up more quickly because I didn't want to frustrate him and risk losing his thirty-something energy, a factor that every company wanting to stay relevant must bring, year in and year out.

Stu and I had several difficult conversations over a period of six to eight months. I wanted him to stay and be a culture ambassador, as well as to continue making new restaurant deals. Our relationship would need mending, and there was no quick fix for that. Both Malnati's and I owed him a big debt for his steady leadership for many years. Yet, while I valued him as my partner and loved him as a person, I felt that this was one of those times when I needed to wear the hat of owner and make what felt like the right call for the future of the company. To people in our company, it must have felt like the time Jerry Krause let Chicago Bulls coach Phil Jackson go. Will anyone ever forgive him for that? That kind of decision can be extremely difficult, because people for whom you care deeply are bound to get hurt. The working relationship that led Malnati's on an incredible run would no longer be the same, even though Stu and I continued to share an office, as we always had.

By 2013, we were approaching the point where we had pretty well saturated our home market, having opened in most of the A sites. Mark would help us move fully into the twenty-first century. Our strength had always been our ability to execute, because our crew was so committed to being the best. But hard work alone would not help us grow our company and give us the ability to build a team outside Chicago. I thought Mark could do that.

Mark insisted that everything be documented. We redid our training manuals and recipe books. We put our standard operating procedures into words. We even hired a consultant to help us document the ingredients we baked into our Malnati culture and then created a system to measure it year over year. We were moving in a direction, and we wanted to make sure our team was following.

For too long, we had remained a company where lessons were primarily passed down in the old-school oral tradition. We could do that because future leaders would incubate for years at Malnati's before they ran anything. We were promoting almost all our managers from within. If their careers were going to unfold here, they would acquire the basics of The Malnati Way by learning from more senior leaders before they became leaders themselves. That pass-it-down mindset was great in the years before we started opening multiple stores each year and opening stores in other states. "What got you here won't get you there!" Dr. Spencer Johnson says in the popular management book *Who Moved My Cheese?* We needed to hire managers from the outside, welcoming them in a friendly way, versus making them break in.

Upgrading our training happened just in time, because by 2014, we were hiring almost two thousand people a year for both newly created positions as well as roles that tend to turn over more quickly—roles such as servers and busboys, dishwashers and phone workers. How do you quickly introduce that many people to a different way of doing things if it's not written down or on videos? Not very well.

There would be no more throwing trainees into the deep water to see which ones could swim, as we had done for years. All our top leaders needed to play a role in training as we sought to professionalize. Best practices were captured and then taught in an organized manner by our best teachers. Our goal was to codify our systems so that our staff could move easily from one store to another, with everyone singing out of the same hymnal.

27.

Our Manager-in-Training (MIT) program sprang from the necessity to have multiple new managers trained and waiting in the wings as we continued to expand into neighborhoods in the Chicagoland area. In Stu's words, we were creating a farm system akin to Major League Baseball's minor leagues. (If a subject didn't have a sports metaphor attached to it, Stu figured it wasn't worth discussing.) Our district managers were tasked with noticing staff members with leadership potential in kitchens and the front of the house of their stores.

We have been blessed with many people who started in the trenches of Malnati's and just needed to be discovered. People don't always know their own potential. Often in our line of work, people come from broken families or from failed marriages and reach out to a business that doesn't require experience, only a willingness to bust your butt and get along with colleagues next to you busting theirs. When many of those hardworking people realize that they are gifted in making others happy by creating fabulous food and/or by serving with friendliness and care, great restaurant people are born. As they bloom, we seek to plug them into leadership roles where their blossoming inspires others. Growing great managers is the most vital ingredient to growing a brand. Malnati's lives and dies by the big and little decisions that a manager makes every day on his or her shift. Staff members love their jobs when they have a fair and encouraging manager. Customers feel seen and appreciated. And the pizza coming out of our kitchen gets all the attention it needs to maintain its extraordinary quality.

Over time, we learned the importance and the difficulty of bringing in people from the outside who could add to our processes with their unique experiences. There were big wins, such as with Bill Sullivan, who started at Malnati's, then became a sommelier at Le Français, the most exclusive French restaurant in Chicagoland, before returning to Lou's to become a partner and district manager. Among other things, Bill used his training to build better wine lists for us and to instill a five-star eye for service detail. Lynn Young's experience with Burger King brought us the ability to stay organized and operate at a high level in tight quarters while never running out of anything.

Many leaders who came from elsewhere fit like a glove. But our success rate was only about half as good when we recruited people from outside Malnati's as when they were homegrown. Sometimes our culture's practice of giving and receiving honest feedback took experienced managers by surprise, and they didn't handle it well at first. If they were willing to trust the process long enough to realize that their colleagues' honesty wasn't meant to hurt but to stretch them, they would almost always become welcome adopters. But, as with transplant surgery, at times there were "tissue rejections" and some new managers did not bond well with Malnati's. This sometimes slowed the growth of our store count, but our primary goal was always community and not rapid expansion.

Restaurant people tend to learn best through experience. The classroom never suited most of us well. We were the kids who got in trouble for talking to classmates when we were supposed to be developing a relationship with the periodic table or photosynthesis. We were more outgoing than other kids, as in outgoing down to the principal's office. While the teacher taught, and we were expected to sit, we wanted to be up doing stuff. Moving. We determined at an early age that we didn't want to spend our lives behind desks. Running between the kitchen and the dining room with a stop at the bar, solving multiple problems at the same time—that is what best suited us.

I keep that in mind when I lead the segment on customer complaints during our MIT program. I colead with Jimmy D'Angelo, our COO, and we try to make the meeting as experiential as possible. By the end, we will have worked up a sweat, laughed a lot, and hopefully passed on a few nuggets from our decades of trying to please customers. To build some kindling for the fire, we ask the trainees about instances when they have been confronted by customers unhappy with the service they received. Memories of times when you've dealt with someone's frustration in the middle of a crowded lobby have a way of lingering in your mind, so we use those most uncomfortable situations as fodder for our role-play exercises.

We talk about the lady who found a Pokémon card in her food; the guy whose wife ordered from Pizza Hut, but he came to our place to pick the order up; the grandma who swore she had a credit from twenty-two years ago that she had misplaced, but still wanted three large pizzas at no charge. In the MIT session, one trainee assumes the role of the irate customer, and another becomes the manager on duty. The rest of the group observes carefully and provides feedback.

Jimmy D. teaches trainees to view every tenuous situation as a high-leverage opportunity to turn someone into a lifetime Malnati disciple. Every aggravated customer wants to be seen and heard, wants to know that their satisfaction matters and that their complaint makes sense. So during training we spend a lot of time emphasizing that how we listen and how we connect to people determines our success or failure. We know that a new manager is likely to be uncomfortable handling conflict and may simply seek to fix the problem. We teach that a too quick "I'm sorry" feels cheap and doesn't accomplish our goal of winning the customer over. We don't want the manager to use a precise script, but to let their empathy flow from their heart. The conversation should sound something like this:

CUSTOMER (fuming): "This is the second time I've received the wrong order!"

MANAGER: "We've messed up on your order again? I would be really frustrated if that happened to me." (Listen and reflect back what the customer said. Letting him know you agree with him demonstrates empathy.)

CUSTOMER: "I AM FRUSTRATED! How do you stay in business making so many stupid mistakes? I like this place, but I'm not going to order from here again."

MANAGER: "Your disappointment makes total sense to me, Mr. Fuller. I am really sorry that this happened, and that it has now happened twice. And I don't blame you for not wanting to order from us again."

CUSTOMER: "My friends all swear by this place. But you don't seem to be able to get it right for me." (Here is your opening. His anger is subsiding, and you are listening for this. He wants to love Lou's, just like his friends, so now you help him.)

MANAGER: "We should be able to get your pizza perfect for you every time. We pride ourselves on excellence, and our kitchen crew has years and years of experience making the best pizza anywhere. I'd like to show you that this was just a fluke if you'd be willing to give us one more chance. Will you?"

CUSTOMER: "I guess I could try one more time. Sure. Your pizza really is outstanding . . ."

MANAGER: "First things first! Can we remake the pizza we botched and send it over to your home right now? Of course, we will refund what you paid." (Err on the side of generosity. If they are eating in our restaurant, pick up the check and bring over dessert as well. If they are a carryout customer, send soda or a frozen pizza along with the new pizza.)

CUSTOMER: "We have to put the kids to bed now, but we gave them something else to eat. We're starving, and a new pizza would be great."

MANAGER: "We will get that to you right away. And will you ask for me personally the next time you order? Or call me on my cell phone in case I'm not working that day so I can babysit your order. Or your kids! I'm going to send you a gift card to make sure you give us another try. I'm really sorry to have ruined your family's meal tonight." (Make sure that a little personal note goes out with that gift card.)

We developed an acronym around pleasing disgruntled customers:

P—Purpose is to win back our guest.

L—Listen and reflect back to the guest until they are feeling heard.

E—Empathy. Put yourself in their shoes.

A—Apologize for our mistake and their inconvenience.

S—Solve. Fix the problem as fast as possible, being creative.

E—Enhance the solution by erring on the side of generosity. Never be cheap in your desire to save Malnati's money. Create an outcome for the customer that exceeds their expectations.

The order of the response is critical. Listening and having empathy must always come before trying to solve or we risk fixing a mistake but still losing a customer.

Lou always preached to his staff that you don't make it long in this business without connecting to your customers. And the time when you have the best chance for that connection is when they are experiencing a problem. This is the precise moment when relationships are created, and our guests gain a name and a face they know they can trust at their neighborhood pizza place.

Working their way through many examples and simulating the pressure of a live experience, our trainees get better and better at handling difficult situations—especially since they are working in front of Jim and me. A manager cannot be great unless they are great at listening and having compassion. It's critical to make sure our trainees learn how to demonstrate their care and adopt the principle that they aren't going to willingly let anyone walk away unhappy from one of our stores.

We tell trainees that building a solid team will determine whether your store stays successful or goes into a tailspin. We teach that during the interview process, you should have a preliminary read on someone you do or don't want to hire after a few minutes. If the applicant is friendly, happy, and shows genuine interest in being a part of Malnati's, they've passed the first hurdle. If they are late for their meeting, seem pessimistic, or describe their last boss in an unsavory manner, a bell should go off in your head. If a few bells go off, the interviewee has flunked what I call the Felony Test—it might be something as trite as their annoying laugh—but you should understand that a minor annoyance can quickly build up until you cringe every time you see or hear them. Trust your gut, and if you have doubts, don't hire them, because within a few short weeks of having them on your staff, you may be doing life in prison without a chance for parole.

To get our trainees to focus on what's important to learn about a potential hire in an interview, we tell them to focus on what has led to their own success. Jimmy and I ask them about their own strong qualities. What led the people who recommended them to think they have Malnati DNA? *Work ethic* and being a *team player* are usually two of the first distinctions the trainees mention. Of course, we expect our leaders to exemplify hospitality and to be honest, dependable, a role model, and so on. But if they don't have those first two, they can manage one of our stores, but they will never truly be a leader in this culture. We tell them that a manager is someone who directs his staff, and the staff listens because they don't have a choice. A *leader* is someone people *choose* to follow whether he or she is a manager or not. And in our crazy kitchens, people follow someone who loves to work their ass off while making it fun for those around them. You can build a pretty good team hiring people like that.

The third component of our DNA is a *commitment to growth*.

Personal growth. Are you willing to stretch yourself by inviting others to speak candidly to you about the challenges you face as you try to grow as a leader? Can you handle that without becoming defensive? We believe in the philosophy that leaders are always learning. John C. Maxwell, one of the country's experts on leadership, once said, "When you're done learning, you're done leading!"

Defining personal growth is no easy task, but I like how Jim Dethmer begins his classic, *The 15 Commitments of Conscious Leadership*. Dethmer is a genius communicator. He can aggregate great material from multiple places and make it take on a far more memorable flavor. He believes that all personal growth is built upon two primary pillars. To paraphrase him:

1. Are you willing to *be curious* or do you have to be right? Will you consider another point of view or are you locked into already "knowing"? It is nearly impossible for people committed to being right to be an effective part of any team.

2. Are you willing to *take 100 percent responsibility* for what occurs in your life, or are you living under the influence of people, places, and things, a victim to the drama that surrounds you? Is life something happening *to you* or is it something authored *by you* and not someone else's fault when challenges occur?

I always end the training session by telling the trainees a story about customer service. It starts with the time our oldest daughter, Kelsey, decided she needed a pair of Doc Martens shoes. Why? Because she was in junior high, and all the cool kids had them! Since she was in the middle of a growth spurt, Jeanne and I told her, "No, it doesn't make sense to spend over one hundred dollars on shoes that you're going to outgrow in about twenty minutes." So what does any self-respecting teen do when Mom and Dad deny her inalienable right to have expensive, cool shoes? Right. She asks Grandma.

But as my mom stepped up to spoil our firstborn that Christmas with a pair of Doc Martens, another acquisition was on a collision course with Kelsey and her new shoes. Jeanne had decided to surprise the family (and her husband) with a little Shih Tzu puppy named Sam. So before bed on Christmas night, Kelsey and I had a talk about puppies and how they like to chew on everything in sight. Being a responsible kid, she showed me a high shelf she had cleaned off in her closet where she would place her new shoes each night so Sam couldn't get to them.

Sure enough, each night as we prayed with her, the shoes were right where she promised they would be . . . until one night that spring when she got home late from basketball practice, had a ton of homework, and crashed at some point between her history textbook and her science project. The next morning, I was greeted by my daughter's tearful words: "The dog ate my shoes. I forgot to put them on the shelf."

Fortunately, at about that same time, I was in counseling learning how to be a better parent (or maybe it was about how not to be such a bad parent). Anyway, one of the lessons was around not losing my *shit completely* in moments like these. Instead, I told her that it was OK and that everyone makes mistakes; the key is to learn from them. Perhaps I didn't say it with quite that degree of serenity.

But, why, you're likely asking yourself, am I telling this story to our MITs?

Sam chowed down in 1993, and a department store called Nordstrom had just opened in a nearby mall. I had been hearing tales of Nordstrom for a while, and I knew it was supposed to have the largest shoe department anywhere. What's more, Nordstrom was proudly famous for having top-notch customer service. I didn't know if my mom had bought the shoes there, but I figured Nordstrom was a good bet to be the place that could repair them. Here was my plan:

We go to Nordstrom and they say they can fix the shoes.

I pay for the repair.

Kelsey agrees to babysit for her little brother and sister on numerous occasions to satisfy her debt.

Bonus—A) Kelsey learns consequences around needing expensive shoes. B) I'm nominated for various parenting awards for using this as a teaching moment and not traumatizing my child.

We found the Nordstrom store amazing! The shoe department appeared to stock twelve million styles. A friendly salesman approached, and I began to explain our situation: Grandma ... Doc Martens ... Shih Tzu ... parenting moment ... Nordstrom repair ... lifelong babysitting ...

The salesman looked at the mangled shoes, nodded his head a few times, and put Kelsey's foot on the silver sizing apparatus. He nodded again, smiled at her, and without saying a word walked away with her Doc Martens. I expected him to pop back from behind the wall and tell us the repair will cost thirty dollars and the shoes will be ready in two weeks. Instead, he emerged with new Doc Martens and placed them on my daughter! I started to stammer, certain that this filthy opportunist was trying to sell me a new pair of this overpriced footwear! I sputtered that he must have misunderstood. So much for the B.S. about the great customer service, I thought.

And then he finally spoke. "Sir, we could repair your daughter's shoes for her and still will if you'd like. But I'm not recommending it, because her feet have grown, and she requires a shoe that's a full size larger." He looked into little Kelsey's eyes, as if she were the most important customer he'd ever had the pleasure to help. "I'm really sorry about what happened with your puppy," he told her. "I'm sure you're a really responsible kid, like your dad said. Would you be OK if Nordstrom bought you a new pair of Doc Martens in a larger size today? These old ones are just too small."

Kelsey jumped up and down with a huge smile on her face, celebrating her ridiculously good fortune. She thanked her new best friend, the Nordstrom sales guy. I would have smiled too, if I wasn't busy picking up my jaw from the floor. What had just happened? Did that guy just give us these shoes? What would become of my parenting moment? The hours of babysitting?

That's when we started buying shoes for all our kids at Nordstrom. Then their clothes. Then shoes and clothes for Jeanne and me, too! We told all our friends. And I told each and every MIT class that ran through Malnati's for the next thirty years. Nordstrom taught me a lesson in erring on the side of generosity. To win us as customers, the store went far above and beyond what I expected. It indeed won our loyalty and made us into Nordstrom disciples forever.

The salesman metaphorically put himself into Kelsey's shoes. He took the time to understand her dilemma. He connected to her. He created a relationship between our family and Nordstrom that has lasted the test of time.

In telling that story, I try to inspire our new leaders to take care of our customers in a way that may at first seem to be ridiculous. But when one of our customers has been inconvenienced by having to wait way too long, she shouldn't have to pay for our mistake, right? That's on us. And so is her next pizza, because we want to give her a chance to see us deliver great service, and we want to leave her with only good thoughts of Malnati's. Top her off with some tiramisu! Do whatever you have to do to turn an unhappy situation into a celebration.

Ultimately, that single pair of shoes was a pretty good investment for Nordstrom. I tell our trainees to spoil our guests like Nordstrom spoiled Kelsey.

Service that goes even farther than the extra mile—that's how a business makes it for fifty years.

28.

Opening a restaurant outside Illinois was something that I had promised Jeanne we wouldn't do until our kids got out of school. That promise grew out of my desire to be more available as a parent than my father had been. I didn't want to pass on that same baton by being on the road constantly. Melissa, our youngest, was twenty-eight and had just gotten married and still I resisted.

But as Lou Malnati's hit age forty-four in 2015, I woke after a nightmare in which some of our biggest Chicago competitors had opened pizzerias in Arizona and beat us to the punch in that market. Arizona was one of our top five markets for shipping our frozen pizzas. It was also home to the Chicago Cubs spring training facility in Mesa, and many people referred to the Phoenix-Scottsdale area as Chicago West. (The mayor of Phoenix later told me that more than 33 percent of the people living there had some sort of roots in the Chicagoland area!)

I hated how I felt when I awoke from that dream, and it made me reconsider the issue. I judged that the pain of seeing someone else open before we did would surpass the pain of doing it ourselves. A few days later I challenged our strategic leadership team to create a plan to expand into the Arizona market by 2016.

Sasha Milosavljevich and I decided that our goal would be to anchor with a restaurant in both Phoenix and Scottsdale. Sasha graduated from the school of engineering at purdue university (Indiana University guys spell purdue with a small "p") and went on to build air traffic control towers for a big contractor. He is a genius builder and problem solver, and he had added *real estate selection* to the expansive list of areas that he was managing for Malnati's. To help us better understand the market, we quizzed local brokers and a multitude of friends and associates who have homes in the Phoenix region. Once the news started leaking out that we planned to open in Arizona, everyone had an opinion on where we should locate, including anyone who had once vacationed in Arizona or even imagined they might visit sometime soon. Among Arizona residents, often the "primo" location that people suggested was within about a mile of where they lived.

One of the most difficult things I've done is to try to fathom the ins and outs of a market in which I've never lived. In Chicago, I understand how traffic patterns work. From a lifetime of experiencing where people like to go and which areas they like to avoid, I found it almost second nature to pick strong locations for Malnati's. Stu and I have watched where businesses last a long time and where there's a lot of turnover. But none of that experiential knowledge comes to play in another state. We could drive around for days, but never have the advantage of living there for years.

Eventually, Sasha and I found the best opportunity in an outdoor mall in Phoenix that was anchored by AJ's Fine Foods, a high-quality grocery chain that has been in Arizona forever. We would be the second restaurant on a property that had parking for hundreds of cars and whose new owners were pouring millions of dollars into the refurbishment and updating of the center. Our store would boast seating for 250 people, with an indoor/outdoor bar, and a fabulous patio fronted by a green space and fountain that would allow kids to play when they tired of sitting. The midcentury modern design that Mark Knauer conceived was fresh and welcoming, and it had the classic look of a restaurant that had been there forever, standing the test of time.

Before we could open, we knew we had to solve the water issue. Chicago's clean, tasty, and abundant Lake Michigan water was perfect for making our dough. But because of Arizona's desert environment, the water there contains a high mineral content. We shipped gallons of AZ water to Chicago for testing, and when we made dough with both Chicago and Arizona water, the Arizona dough looked darker and didn't taste the same.

So Sasha and his team built a reverse-osmosis mini-filtration plant in the restaurant that would remove some of the chemicals and create water that virtually replicated Lake Michigan. It worked like a charm—until it didn't!

We made a deal with our purveyors to get our Midwest cheese and sausage delivered on a weekly basis. Then we talked Big Mike Sterner into moving his family out there so he could assume the role of market partner. An offensive lineman in college, Mike had started at Malnati's as a bartender after the NFL showed a lack of interest. He had grown into a great store manager and then district manager because he worked hard, he cared about people, and his staff loved him. We were convinced that we could successfully build out our culture in Arizona around Mike. Then Bernie Pechtel, the GM who had operated Chicago's busiest store, asked to go, and we knew that we'd be starting with an outstanding nucleus to build around.

We were lucky enough to recruit a great staff as well. Some of our frontline people living in Arizona had worked at Malnati's in Chicago at some point, and that also helped to transport our culture and values to Phoenix. I remember standing in front of the entire assembled team just before we threw open the doors to the public for the first time on a summer day in 2016. I told the team what a milestone this was for us as a company. I shared my hope that the principles of work ethic, teamwork, and a willingness to support one another—factors that had been so critical to success in Chicago—would prove to be equally valued there.

Then Jeanne and I passed out a tiny pewter heart to each team member. The hearts were an idea that Jeanne and our daughters came up with on a trip to South Africa. Just before leaving, they bought a handful of these little silver mementos, and they decided to pass them out to people they met who seemed to need a reminder that they were loved. The reactions to this small but meaningful gift were so positive that they decided to found a movement called *SpreadingHearts.org*. Back in the states, they located an artist who designed the hearts and stamped them with their new logo. We gave each of our staff one heart to keep for themselves as a reminder that we see them and appreciate them, and another to hand to one of our new guests who appeared to need a little cheering up. That set the tone for the kind of welcoming, caring environment that we wanted our group to feel and to extend to others.

By opening day, the word had spread, and ex-Midwesterners showed up from all over the desert, some driving as far as three hours to feast on the Chicago delicacy they had been missing. For several weeks, people waited for more than two hours to get out of the sun and into the bar, where they still had to wait another hour to be seated. We set up water stations outside so our guests wouldn't dehydrate. One local television reporter took a helicopter over our location to show the lines snaking through the mall. As he flew, he munched on deep-dish and told his audience that it was worth the wait. Our guests were famished by the time they sat down, but they left satisfied, usually having ordered so much food that they would be eating out of their doggie bags for a week! While dining, many shared their memories of important occasions in their past they had spent at Malnati's in Chicago.

Jeanne and I again moved into a nearby apartment so that I could spend as many hours as necessary in the store during that critical first month. For this first out-of-state opening, Rick and Tina brought my mom out in her wheelchair so she could help in the celebration. Scott and Carolyn Weiner came as well to share in what was a momentous occasion for Lou Malnati's. Jeanne and Jarrett Stevens, our faithful friends and pastors at the Soul City Church in the West Loop, also made the trip so they could pray with us over the new venture as they had at many of our prior grand openings.

In those first months, we repeatedly had to patch up our kitchen crew, as it took a huge effort to keep up with the crowds, and some staffers didn't want to bring it day after day. On top of that, we had issues with the dough, partly related to the water and partly to the lack of humidity in Arizona summers. Dough issues are five-alarm problems in the pizza business, and though we were able to sort them out quickly, they did produce multiple nights of no sleep. Fortunately, we had a strong group of Chicago veterans, and our Chicago DMs, such as Eloy and Schrager, returned twice for stints to work with the new kitchen crew and get us through the hectic extended honeymoon. We did almost $1.5 million in sales over our first thirty days.

29.

I TURNED SIXTY IN THE fall of 2015, and though I was healthy and still liked my work, I knew that it was time to create a succession plan. I had always been focused on building a team and growing people. We had reinvested profits into new restaurants year after year, and the balance sheet looked strong. Our fledgling company had taken off its training wheels long ago, and now it had significant value. Was it time to bring in an investor/financial partner to provide some liquidity?

I realized that I was thinking about the potential value more than I wanted to. It hung right in front of me, dangling in my consciousness, so close that it was popping up almost every day. I didn't want to think about it, but I didn't want to look back a few years later and feel the shame around missing the boat on a bull market that might never return. The company faced one of those Y's in the road, like a dice player on a long run with lots of money on the table. Do you keep rolling or do you pick up your chips? I felt responsible, and I didn't want to blow it for my family, for my brother's family, or for anyone else associated with Malnati's who stood to reap the benefits.

Years before, when I was only twenty-five, I had come upon one of those Y's. Along with that fork in the road came the old saying, "Pigs get fed, and hogs get slaughtered." The line had stuck with me as a reminder not to be greedy. It told me of the importance of recognizing when you're getting your fair share and acknowledging the value of not always pushing for more or insisting on having more right now. I needed to remind myself of an adage like that because I love bigger and better.

In 1980, we brought deep-dish pizza to England, and Jeanne and I were in our first year of marriage. While on the flight home from our grand opening, my mom, who was traveling with us, got bumped up to first class and was seated next to an engaging older gentleman. She boasted that Malnati's was about to take England by storm because we make the most incredible pizza you could imagine.

When I went to check on her, the man beside her introduced himself as Charlie Lubin, whom I knew to be the baking genius responsible for the delicious line of coffee cakes that my mom always had in our refrigerator. Over the past thirty years, he had built a brand named after his daughter Sara Lee. And now my mother had gotten Charlie all pumped up about our pizza! Charlie fri*#cken Lubin! She even persuaded him to write out his recipe for his all-butter coffee cake on the back of a cocktail napkin.

True to his word, Charlie called the next week, and I brought some pizzas up to his new, state-of-the-art Sara Lee kitchen world headquarters in north suburban Deerfield. He loved the taste and the look of our pizza. A few weeks later, he invited me to a meeting with him and a few of his friends downtown at The Standard Club. Two of the friends were Edwin Hokin, CEO of the shipping supply company Unarco, and Jerry Reinsdorf, CEO of the Balcor real estate company and soon to be the owner of the Chicago White Sox and the Chicago Bulls.

Charlie made no small plans, and we discussed the possibility of turning Malnati's into a national brand. The businessmen at the table sounded enamored with the idea, and I was blown away that they could have so much confidence in our product. Charlie invited me to Deerfield a few more times to experiment with both fresh and frozen pizzas. He had pioneered the process of baking and selling Sara Lee's coffee cakes in aluminum pans, as well as freezing fully cooked products directly after baking to ensure freshness. Charlie thought Lou Malnati's pizza might respond well to a similar baking/freezing process.

But as I dug closer into the deal that Charlie was offering, I realized that he and his pals would put up the money for expansion, and Malnati's would do the work to build the brand. When I asked Charlie how much of the newly formed company we would still own and who would make the critical decisions, he quoted me his Golden Rule: "He who has the gold, makes the rules!"

So here's how the Y stood: At age twenty-five, I could have all the capital necessary to attempt to create a national brand; or we could nurse our little business along, stay in relative obscurity, and hope we could cobble something meaningful together a little at a time. And that's precisely when Scott Weiner's older brother Jack whispered to me, "Pigs get fed, and hogs get slaughtered." If I were to be a hog and needed to have it all right then, I might live to regret it—particularly if Malnati's grew fast using our hard work and Sara Lee money, but our family owned only a small piece of it. I decided that the life that I had was just fine, and that I'd take my chances working for myself rather than for the guys who had the gold.

Now, thirty-five years later, a lot had changed. The business had grown slowly and methodically, but Malnati's had reached some forty-five locations and was doing $150 million in sales annually. Not expanding before our people were ready had been our mantra, but suddenly I realized that we had become a good-sized company despite the deliberate pace with which we opened new stores. The trick to our success was not to open new stores faster; it was to not close any of the ones we opened. It was about investing time in building a strong foundation under each unit before the team left to open another one. Our little company had achieved real value. Still, I had started to feel as if I was reaching the twilight of my restaurant career.

I tried once again to persuade Will to consider moving back to Chicago to make a career at Malnati's. But he had opened two restaurants in Manhattan's Chelsea neighborhood, and it was quickly burning him out. He had begun to build a podcast production company called At Will Media, in which he found far more passion than he ever did in the restaurant business. He would eventually leave the restaurant business, and today Will and his team sell original content podcasts to the likes of Apple TV+ and Amazon with the hope that many will be adapted into TV shows. Will and his talented wife, Alissa, a fashion executive and author, and our grandson Remy still live in New York City. Kelsey enjoyed being an educator and wasn't interested in the restaurant business; neither was Melissa, who, like her mom, was called to be a social worker. Our kids had all found their niche, but nobody wanted to work in the business in which my grandfather, my father, and my brother and I had thrived.

So it happened that Mark Agnew and I were having lunch outdoors in Wilmette in July 2016 after spending most of the past two months in Phoenix opening that store. Though the opening had gone well, I was tired. I loved the outcome, but I'm not a fan of being so far away from home for long periods. I think Mark and I were walking through the current issues in the business when I stopped the conversation and said, "Mark, I think I'm ready to bring in a financial partner to buy a stake in Malnati's." Having restaurants in other states sounded sexy, but it was risky to expand outside of Chicago, and I found myself desiring to be more conservative with both our money and my energy. I felt myself hitting the wall, and I knew I didn't want to work like that for much longer.

Mark had heard me allude to this before, but this time he knew I was serious. The market for evaluating businesses of our size was experiencing never-before-seen "multiples." We had watched Dick Portillo sell out of his Portillo's hot dog empire for nearly $1 billion, a multiple of thirteen times Portillo's adjusted annual profits. For most of my lifetime, those multiples had typically resided in the six-to-eight-times neighborhood. I wasn't quite ready to stop working, but I was fairly confident that multiples wouldn't remain at that level forever. I reasoned that on our own, we could potentially have a fabulous next five years, but then when we went to find a partner, the multiples would have receded, and we would have worked for five years and created no additional value.

Later that day, we called Mark's contact Chip Dunn from the local merchant bank BDT & Company. We thought he could advise us in locating a partner interested in making a quiet, private investment. Our team was solid, and the plan would be for the Malnati team to continue to run the company as we saw fit without interference. Given the cost of opening our first store in Phoenix, we knew we'd need to bring in outside capital for further out-of-state expansion. I was sixty, and it didn't make sense for me (and Rick, who was still my financial partner) to take on that much risk.

We now had forty stores in the Chicago area. When Phoenix opened so strong, we knew we were proving out a test case for how far deep-dish pizza could take us. Anyone looking to invest with us would need to place high value on the out-of-state expansion opportunity.

BDT had a reputation for supporting family businesses across the globe, supplying counsel and capital. Because the firm was headquartered in Chicago, it seemed to be the perfect organization to lean into for support. We told Chip the number at which we thought we would be comfortable doing a deal, and he thought we were on target and that BDT could help find a partner. But when he called back, he said that BDT would be interested in becoming our partner. Mark and I both loved that we might be able to wrangle something quickly and without a lot of fanfare.

About two weeks later, Chip arranged a meeting in the firm's offices in the Equitable Building. He and the team at BDT had done an assessment of the value of Malnati's and had prepared an offer. Mark and I came with Rick and Keith Cantrell, who had founded a boutique firm that specialized in providing families with a suite of financial and advisory services. Keith and I had served together on the finance team at Soul City Church, and Keith had quickly become a trusted friend and advisor. Representing BDT were Chip, legal counsel Rob Verigan, and the principal and namesake of the firm, Byron David Trott. Trott had started his own firm after leaving his post as vice chairman of investment banking at Goldman Sachs after a twenty-seven-year career there.

As BDT began to walk us through key points in the proposal they had prepared, I skipped ahead to the end and saw that they were valuing Malnati's at less than the figure we had provided to them when we spoke earlier about BDT representing us. I sat quietly for a minute or two, and then, not attempting to hide my frustration, I said, "You knew our number. If you weren't going to hit it, you should have warned us before you made us come down to your office." And with that, we walked out of the room.

The next day, Byron Trott called to ask for a one-on-one meeting. He apologized and said that the firm was still interested in Malnati's and that *he* was the best partner for a growing, high-potential business like ours. He said that BDT would be different from traditional private equity firms that resell businesses in five to seven years, because BDT typically stays in partnerships with their portfolio companies for twelve to fifteen years and oftentimes longer. I told him I would call him back.

Agnew had another contact, this one at Madison Dearborn Partners, another Chicago private equity firm. We sent our financials and gave the firm until the end of the week to make an offer. We also set a valuation figure that was substantially higher than the one we had given BDT. Our rationale was that we needed to know how high we could go because we didn't want to leave anything on the table. Madison Dearborn was very interested.

We met the Madison Dearborn guys on a Friday and had a cordial meeting. They had put a team to work on estimating the value of Malnati's, and the team hadn't slept for three days. Though the MD representatives said the firm wanted to be our partner, they couldn't get the numbers to work to give us what we were asking. In the end, Madison Dearborn offered slightly less than BDT had. That wasn't the best outcome, but at least it told us that we were in the ballpark with our assumptions.

I returned Byron Trott's call and we had dinner in a corner booth at Shaw's Crab House downtown. I found Byron to be charming. He could sell gas to a guy with a Tesla. He was charismatic in a way that made me believe that the two of us would be best friends forever. But this meeting was about getting the best possible deal to sell part of Malnati's, and after we had eaten, I told him that the deal I was offering was slightly less than what I had originally told Chip, but $15 million more than they had recently offered. He swallowed hard but said yes.

The next few weeks were crazy, as we negotiated the fine points of the deal. Agnew and Kori Pierce, our director of finance who could mesh a thousand details and make sense of them at any given time, did a masterful job of pulling together all the documents and navigating through the due diligence, often working until three or four in the morning. There were so many points at which that deal could have fallen apart, but Mark and Kori kept it on track.

As a result, we were able to help twenty-five of our core leaders to become stock partners in Malnati's—twenty-five who had earned the right through their commitment to the company. We also shared some of the proceeds with every member of our team who had been with us for ten years or more, many of whom had retired.

Over a three-week period, I set up individual meetings with 330 different individuals who had virtually no idea why I wanted to talk to them privately. When we met, I told them about taking on a PE partner, but if they were still working, not to worry about losing their job. I thanked them for their contribution to the growth of the company. And just as their trepidation about coming to our meeting was subsiding and they had stopped sweating, I handed them a check. In total, we wrote checks for $7 million, and our people could take the trip they had always dreamed about or buy a car or simply pay off credit card debt—however they wanted to use the payout. Those who had invested much of their lives making sure our guests experienced friendliness and great food deserved to benefit.

30.

After our deal closed, I saw Byron at a few different BDT functions, but he was off frying bigger fish. He assigned one of his key guys to be the point person from BDT, but he was inexperienced in the restaurant business. He was intelligent, but we didn't see eye-to-eye strategically on the important issues that our company was facing. He wanted to open lots of stores quickly to build the top line. I began to understand that the business model of private equity is different from ours. PE firms need to produce enterprise growth along with a regular, dependable return for their investors.

The restaurant business is not all that predictable, and at different times in our long history, we experienced unpredictable swings in year-over-year sales and profits. That occurred in 2017 and 2018 as we added units, but since our labor costs were rising, we didn't see much of an increase in earnings. Malnati's has traditionally found that as long as we pay extra attention to the fundamentals of friendly service and perfect pizza, we can weather any storm and ultimately continue to grow. Private equity takes a shorter-term, less patient approach and wants to reach for levers to steady the ship right away. Levers that don't always exist.

BDT wanted more answers faster, and I could see that this constant need for reporting and explanation was making it difficult for Mark Agnew, who became our CEO after the transaction. He had to invest enormous effort to deal with BDT while at the same time trying to manage the company. When Mark called me about two years into the new partnership to say he couldn't do it anymore, I was hardly surprised. He and I went back and forth for months. He even said he was considering moving out of the country for a year to provide his four kids the experience of attending school in Spain. In January 2019, just days before he claimed he planned to announce his retirement, he had a seizure and was rushed to the hospital. He called to tell me he had been diagnosed with a brain tumor. I couldn't believe what I was hearing.

Coincidentally, after we had sold part of the interest in Malnati's to BDT, our family had decided to make a gift to Northwestern Medicine that would result in the naming of the Lou and Jean Malnati Brain Tumor Institute as a focal point of the Lurie Comprehensive Cancer Center. The gift had a personal dimension. Years before, Dr. James Chandler, the most tenured neurosurgeon in Chicago, had done surgery on my mom's spine, and afterward she had adopted him into our family. Our gift helped to guarantee Dr. Chandler and his team funding to recruit some of the top researchers and doctors in the world and facilitated the creation of a much larger and cutting-edge facility on the twentieth floor of Galter Pavilion at Northwestern. Incredibly, the new institute opened on the day after the night Mark had his seizure. It was clearly not our plan, but could it really have been an accident that my company's CEO became the first patient at the Malnati Brain Tumor Institute? I don't believe in accidents like that.

Dr. Chandler performed surgery on Mark's tumor the following week, and Dr. Roger Stupp, the chief of neuro-oncology, took over to nurse him back to health. Brain cancer is the hardest cancer to treat because of the difficulty in getting medicine through the blood-brain barrier that shields the brain from toxic substances in the blood. Mark's recovery lasted months, requiring him to relearn motor skills and to recover his vocabulary. Five years later, he is doing well, teaching at the University of Chicago's Booth School of Business and speaking nationally on business topics. Would he have gone through with a resignation from his dream job at Malnati's? I don't really know.

Mark's need for a long, focused time for rehabilitation meant we had to find another leader for Malnati's. My preference, as always, was to promote someone from inside the company. But Byron Trott argued that we should enroll a search firm and explore outside options. Ultimately, we agreed that bringing in someone from the outside would give us an opportunity to have a leader who had already been down the growth path that Malnati's needed to walk.

Early in 2020, the search led us to my long-ago acquaintance Mike Archer. Nationally regarded for his ability to understand financial nuance from the perspective of operational expertise, he was a solid choice. After a twenty-five-year career that included developing Sullivan's Steakhouse and stints as COO for Del Frisco's, president of TGI Friday's, and CEO of Houlihan's, Archer returned to his hometown Chicago and became the CEO of Malnati's. All those years after we had first met at Chicago-Fest, things had come full circle.

It seemed as if twenty minutes after he accepted and moved his family to Lincoln Park the COVID-19 pandemic broke out in the United States. Before he could even make a first visit to all the Chicago-area stores, we were facing business challenges that no one had experienced before. Taking staffers' temperatures, trying to work while staying six feet away from one another, wearing masks, closing dining rooms, moving service to outdoor tents. The memories are still haunting. All of us had to be careful, had to try to protect our people, while becoming innovative enough to keep our businesses open. Mike was tasked with meeting our existing leadership under conditions far from favorable while pushing quickly for radical changes in this major crisis.

The pizza business had an edge over other restaurants. We were carryout and delivery experts. When the dining rooms were largely closed in Chicagoland from March 2020 until June 2021, our customers could still get our food. Within forty-eight hours, we implemented curbside pickup, a service that could easily have taken months to install in sixty stores. Our carryout and delivery business was stronger than ever and provided jobs for most of our staff. We were able to send repeated financial assistance to those staff members who were unable to work because they were caring for exposed family members or had their own health constraints.

The biggest winner was our shipping business. Tastes of Chicago went wild during COVID-19. As Chicagoans camped out around the country, they needed their Lou's fix. "Send us a six-pack in Montana!" With restaurant dining rooms shut down nationwide, people ventured onto the internet to augment their local choices with delicacies from Chicago. Our sales tripled and, even better, our restaurant cooks, who would otherwise have been furloughed, went to work in our plant making frozen pizzas. We couldn't make pizzas and ship them out fast enough to satisfy the demand. We had to rent temporary fulfillment space because we couldn't handle the volume in our existing warehouse.

While other restaurateurs were fighting for their financial lives, our bottom line remained healthy because of Tastes of Chicago and the e-commerce side hustle that Rick had dreamed up in 1989. Our profits were up in 2020 and about the same in 2021. Although it was tempting, we didn't take the $10 million from the Paycheck Protection Program that the government offered because we already had access to cash. Some people said we were foolish not to take it, because we would never have to pay it back. But other businesses needed it, and we did not.

To me, integrity dictated that Malnati's would always try to do what was right. My parents taught us that the true test of character is what you do when nobody's looking. I remember my father telling me a story about when he was working downtown at Pizzeria Due and a fire started at a nearby restaurant. Once the fire department cleared, Lou stopped dinner service and sent his whole crew over to his neighbor's place, and they carried boxes and boxes of food, alcohol, and miscellaneous items back to Due and held it there for days until his friend's place could reopen. That decision was influenced by character and not by money. He did what was right, even though it cost him.

31.

MALNATI'S FIFTIETH ANNIVERSARY FELL DURING the tail end of the pandemic. Not being able to throw a giant party on St. Patrick's Day of 2021 disappointed our entire team. It was probably most disappointing for my ninety-one-year-old mother, otherwise known as Mama Malnati. She has always been a great cheerleader, leading the charge to celebrate our achievements and the growth of the company. Plus, she loves a big party, an opportunity to bring on the champagne garnished with sliced peaches. One full year into the COVID-19 era, everyone was tired from the toll that masking and social distancing were taking in our dining rooms, kitchens, and everywhere else.

Most of our management meetings had moved to Zoom. Our stores remained linked, and Jimmy D. and Mike Archer communicated the daily and weekly tweaks and government public health rules. Members of our home office didn't come in nearly as much due to safety concerns. Zoom helped us maintain some sort of connection, when connection had become risky. The solid relationships among people who had worked together for twenty or thirty years before COVID-19 clearly acted as a glue that helped hold the whole thing together.

I felt and still feel so much gratefulness for having made it to the milestone of fifty years. Gratefulness for the team that I was privileged to know and love and work alongside, most of them for the biggest slice of their careers (pun intended). I worked with people who treated Malnati's as their own, who never needed to be asked to stay late or to cover a shift. They just did it, and they did it without fanfare. I worked with people who went through hell in their personal lives but reached out to their team for the support they needed and never let it affect their job. I worked with people who never made a day of my career feel like work. Love for your team evokes loyalty. Loyalty creates a spirit of ownership and kindness that is palpable and registers easily with a coworker or a guest. Create that, and you've established a firm foundation.

A few months after our fiftieth anniversary and just short of our fifth anniversary of working together, BDT sold its interest in our company to a private investment firm named the Meritage Group, part of the Jim Simons family office. The restaurant business has been up and down since the crisis brought on by COVID-19. Pressure on commodities and labor have caused restaurant and grocery store prices to rise at an unprecedented rate. At the same time, inflation has forced many families to pull back on the number of times they eat out each month. Though Malnati's continues to thrive, other restaurants that were not able to open their dining rooms learned how to prepare their food for carryout or delivery. That created a big change in our industry. Suddenly, delivery services such as DoorDash, Grubhub, and Uber Eats were partnering with restaurants that never considered delivering their food before. The niche that had previously been dominated by pizza and Chinese food became critical to almost every restaurant. That is good news for food delivery options, but the group we compete against to send hot food to your home has grown immensely, and we're working harder now to keep that part of our business growing.

I remain chairman of the board at Malnati's, but I am taking more time to spend with Jeanne and our family. We remain as meticulous as ever about our pizza, and our people are still busting their humps to make our guests happy every day. Though it is sad when I see some of our longtime staff members retire, I know that they have all done a good job passing down the culture of care and concern that makes Malnati's a great company. Meantime, our new generation of leaders is maintaining the attention to detail that has always made us a favorite dining option.

As Malnati's moves into its next fifty years, we can never forget that the essential ingredient is the roster of people with whom we surround ourselves and knowing where we stand in our relationships. In medieval warfare, the soldier who was the standard-bearer acted as a visual beacon for a military unit. During hand-to-hand combat, it was easy to get turned around, so to reorient himself, a soldier could always look up and see where the standard-bearer was positioning his flag. A military unit that maintained cohesion by fighting side by side without being divided by the opposition was far more effective. It's not all that different with a business.

Our standard-bearer has been our Relational Business Model. We believe that people who work on the same team must be meticulous about keeping their relationships clear by not withholding their feelings and being willing to share their full truth. We believe that it's the entire team's responsibility to push for and create resolution of conflict in every relationship on their team. When we take the time to do that and people are reoriented, then the actual business that the team needs to conduct will go smoothly. If the relationships aren't right, the business will suffer. And by suffer, I mean that our guests will sense the discord and even taste the frustration. It's no little thing in the restaurant business.

The Group circles are foundational to who we are and to the community we have sought to create. The circles build trust. Every four weeks, your circle is a home for courage, where we share the intimacy of our feelings on a deep, personal level to let others know who we really are. Trust is built by having grace for one another when we are willing to show our not-so-pretty underbellies; when we disclose the life events that have shaped us for good and bad; when we share the impact that our fellow staffers are having on us, even when we think that they won't be happy to hear it. Sharing our truth builds stronger relationships, even though it's easy to imagine that it would have the opposite effect. Letting our guard down and allowing our real self to show up attracts others because it's authentic, and there is nothing more trustworthy than authenticity.

I think back sometimes to the night I was sitting next to my dad's hospital bed, and we had our final conversation. What would he think about how the company has evolved? These days, I can hear him say, "You did a nice job, Son." At another point in my life, I probably would have imagined him saying, "You did OK, but I would've had four hundred stores opened by now." Fortunately, I have evolved to know that neither message actually comes from Lou. Both are just me, putting my own judgments back on myself but hanging them on Lou. I'm glad that the one that I hear now doesn't feel disparaging. And it's no longer filled with *shoulds*, as in, "You SHOULD do it MY WAY!"

It's just: "You did a nice job." I've learned that's enough to fill my bucket.

I realize that I am far more like Lou than I ever wanted to admit. I think the same thoughts and sometimes I even use the same language. What's different is that I continue to do the hard emotional work to strengthen the relationships I have with my wife and kids. Fortunately for me, they have had the grace to forgive me for the times I wasn't the most available father or the most doting husband. Jeanne and I have been married for nearly fifty years now and should probably start working on the sequel to this story—*The First Fifty Years of Marriage!*

Another thing I've realized now that time has passed is that no one was ever leaving *me*. Not my dad, my brother, or my son. My dad was dying. Rick and Will were finding their ways into careers that they loved and gave them purpose. I may have been narcissistic enough to believe it was about me, but it never was.

Maybe Lou would even have grown to like the Group circles and the therapy work. Maybe he eventually would have seen his way clear to unravel his relationship with his own dad, who had left him alone in Italy as a boy. Or to rebuild his marriage with my mom, who was more than worthy of his love and appreciation. The thing that is crystal clear to me right now is that without the dysfunction in our home, I would never have sought out the counseling that helped me learn to share my feelings. I wouldn't have sought out Rich Blue and others to show me how to resolve conflict in my life.

I see now that God had a plan for me that has taken the things that were broken in my family of origin and used them to show His incredible ability to build something great with damaged parts. To turn coal into diamonds. If not for my need to seek counseling, Malnati's never would have birthed a culture that provided the critical emotional lessons to a team that came together and led a restaurant business to thrive for more than fifty years.

The voice of my father that rang loudly inside my head for years after his passing is now something I've grown to appreciate. He was driven, and his voice helped mold Rick and me into men who wouldn't settle for mediocrity. He wasn't always available, but he was determined to grow his company, and there were no limits to how hard he was willing to work to become successful. His work ethic was a valuable model. He was a tireless promoter, and though that sometimes came out loud and flashy, he was determined to bring others along to share in his success. There was much good that came along with the challenges he created in our family.

Without that bit of unsteadiness in my early years, I wouldn't have turned my car around on the way to the sporting goods store in Bloomington and heeded God's voice, a voice that called me to trust Him. Over these fifty years, He has blessed Malnati's beyond comprehension. He allowed us to fail miserably in Flossmoor, and because of that, we learned the importance of site selection and the necessity of caution when changing anything (such as the ovens) that might alter the pizza.

He helped us repay an astounding amount of debt and resuscitate the business. He brought us a world-class team of people and found a way for us to buy restaurant properties when we weren't even close to being bankable. He used the recession to bring us to the Gold Coast, directed us to the forgotten basement of the Wrigley Building and brought us Coach Gordon so we could open in North Lawndale. He was there with the Malnati Brain Tumor Institute for the very day Mark Agnew needed surgery.

And most wonderfully, He brought the beautiful college girl who had scorned my offer of a free milkshake back to me to become my incredible wife!

Fifty years is just a drop in the bucket to Him.

ACKNOWLEDGMENTS

THOUGH THEY WERE NOT MENTIONED by name in the pages of this story, Malnati's was blessed with hundreds of all-star individuals that gave the best years of their lives to build the culture of our company. I first began to list each person using lists of current team members, as well as those retired or deceased. On my third attempt, I had written more than 300 names.

I had a sinking feeling that I was likely missing another fifty or more, and I just didn't want to hurt anyone that I might have left off the list. You all know who you are, and I celebrate you for doing all the little things that made our company great for generations.

Thank you from the bottom of my heart. I will always be in your debt.

I'd also like you to thank my editor, Richard Babcock, who worked tirelessly to smooth out all the rough edges. I didn't make it easy on him.

I appreciate my publishers, Doug and Jane Seibold, for taking the time to answer this first-time author's endless list of questions, for doing the tedious work to get this book to the finish line, and for actually making it look professional.

My mother, Mama Malnati is 95, and since her vision is not what it once was, I got to spend several nights reading aloud to her, eventually earning her approval. Her memory is still incredible, and she added several terrific anecdotes to the story.

Thanks to my brother, Rick, for the kind introduction, and for his partnership. He is a genius ideator, and a fierce motivator.

Jeanne was there for me day after day, listening, proofreading, rewriting, and pushing me to keep going. My five adult kids all read my drafts, and gave me their feedback which was priceless.

The night before I submitted my final revision, the six of them surprised me by sitting me down and opening a bottle of Caymus Cabernet, my favorite. They proceeded to take turns reading back to me their favorite passages, and explaining why they chose the ones they did. I cried all the way through the process, and told them it was the greatest day of my life.

There were two reasons I first sat down to write this story. I hoped it would become something that current Malnati's staff members would read to learn about the people and the work that went into building our company. I hoped it might help them to be reminded of the principles that have been our guiding lights, and to hang onto the ones that remain useful.

And secondly, I wanted our grandkids and their children to hear the Lou Malnati's story through the words of their Gramps.

If I can accomplish those two things, it will have been worth all the investment of time over the past three years.